MW00650811

MiG-35/D
'Fulcrum' F

Towards the Fifth Generation

HUGH HARKINS

Copyright © 2016 Hugh Harkins

All rights reserved.

ISBN: 1-903630-60-6
ISBN-13: 978-1-903630-60-0

MiG-35/D
'Fulcrum' F

Towards The Fifth Generation

© Hugh Harkins 2016

Published by Centurion Publishing
United Kingdom

ISBN 10: 1-903630-60-6
ISBN 13: 978-1-903630-60-0

This volume first published in 2016

The Author is identified as the copyright holder of this work under sections
77 and 78 of the Copyright Designs and Patents Act 1988

Cover design © Centurion Publishing & Createspace

Page layout, concept and design © Centurion Publishing

All rights reserved. No part of this publication may be reproduced, stored in
a retrieval system, transmitted in any form, or by any means, electronic,
mechanical or photocopied, recorded or otherwise, without the written
permission of the Publisher

The Publisher and Author would like to thank all organisations and services for their
assistance and contributions in the preparation of this volume. JSC RAC (Russian
Aircraft Corporation), PJSC UAC (United Aircraft Corporation), JSC Sukhoi Design
Bureau (Sukhoi Aviation Holding Company), JSC Klimov, JSC Tactical Missiles
Corporation, JSC Concern Radio-Electronic Technologies (KRET), JSC
Ramenskoye Design Bureau (RPKB), NPP Zvezda, Phazotron NIIR, JSC SPC CPR
(JSC Scientific and Production Corporation Precision Instrumentation Systems),
MKPK Avionica, Rostec Corporation and the Ministry of Defence of the Russian
Federation

CONTENTS

INTRODUCTION   i

1 DESIGN LINEAGE – FIRST GENERATION MiG-29   1

2 THE UNIFIED FIGHTER FAMILY   19

3 MiG-35/D DESIGN AND EVOLUTION   27

4 ADVANCED WEAPON OPTIONS   71

5 APPENDICES   83

6 GLOSSARY   85

INTRODUCTION

The RAC MiG-35/D multirole combat aircraft emerged in 2007 as a land based variant of the Unified Fighter Family based on the MiG-29K/KUB naval optimised multirole combat aircraft contracted by the Indian Navy. The MiG-35/D builds on the capabilities of the MiG-29K/KUB and its land based analogue, the MiG-29M/M2, by introducing a number of fifth generation targeting and navigation systems. The introduction of Omni-directional nozzles for the engines will allow the aircraft, like its rivals from Sukhoi, the Su-30MKI series and the Su-35S, to truly enter the realm of 'super-manoeuvrable' flight.

This volume briefly outlines the aircraft design lineage – the first generation MiG-29, and briefly covers the evolution of the Unified Fighter Family of MiG-29K/KUB/MiG-29M2 before moving over to the MiG-35/D which is described in detail. The weapons cleared for the MiG-35/D are described while appendices include specifications on the MiG-35/D and its forebears.

All technical information used in this volume regarding the aircraft, systems and weapons has been furnished by the respective design houses, as has the majority of the photographs and diagrams supporting the text.

1

DESIGN LINEAGE – FIRST GENERATION MiG-29

The origins of the 21st century 4th++ Generation RAC MiG-35/D multi-functional fighter aircraft go back to the Mikoyan Project 9 (MiG-29A), the prototype of which conducted its maiden flight on 6 October 1977.

The design origins of the Project 9 go back to the late 1960's. When intelligence on the projected FX (Fighter Experimental) program aimed at finding a replacement for the McDonnell Douglas F-4 Phantom II, then the USAF main air superiority fighter aircraft, which emerged as the McDonnell Douglas (now Boeing) F-15 Eagle, that was under development for the USAF (United States Air Force), filtered through to the Soviet Union in the late 1960's, it had become clear that a new generation of fighter aircraft possessing high power and manoeuvrability would be required to counter the new American air superiority fighter aircraft. The then current generation of Soviet fighter aircraft such as the MiG-21 would, it was clear, be seriously outclassed by the new American fighter, and the more modern MiG-23 variable-geometry (swing wing) fighter, whilst possessing high performance in regards to areas such as speed, lacked acceptable levels of manoeuvrability.

A number of Soviet Design Bureau commenced design work on new 4th generation air superiority fighter aircraft programs in 1969, initially under the PFI (Advanced Front Line Fighter) aircraft program, the aim of which was to field the Soviet Union's 4th generation fighter aircraft, which, it was hoped, would enter service in the early 1980's. A number of concepts were studied, various designs being drawn up by the design houses of A.I. Mikoyan, P.O. Sukhoi, and A.S. Yakovlev during 1971-1972. The two former design houses were designing high agility aircraft, both arriving at similar configurations, attributed to the fact that both were apparently utilising data from the same research agency. The design that eventually became the PFI Project 9, therefore, resembled, at least, superficially, a scaled down version of the Sukhoi T-10, the latter being designed around a highly blended fore-body and high lift ogive wing with LERX (Leading Edge Root Extensions).

In 2016, RAC is pinning its fighter manufacturing future, certainly for the next decade or so, on the Unified Fighter Family which encompasses the MiG-29K/KUB/MiG-29M/M2 and the MiG-35/D above. RAC

The initial design for the T-10 was complete by September 1971, submitted in February 1972, and, following a preliminary review, design revisions were incorporated, following which full-scale development commenced. As it became increasingly clear that the heavy air superiority fighter for the Soviet IA-PVO (*Istrebitelnaya Aviatsiya Protivo-Vozdushnoy Obstrany*/Air Defence Force) would be built by Sukhoi, Mikoyan looked to downsize its design as it looked to a lightweight fighter role, which emerged in an ex-post-facto requirement for an LFI (*Legikiy Frontovoy Istrebitel* – Light Front line Fighter) issued in 1972, development of the T-10 for the heavy air superiority role going forward in conjunction with development of a lightweight fighter by Mikoyan; the MiG-29 (Project 9), to replace Sukhoi Su-7 ground attack aircraft and MiG-21 lightweight fighter aircraft in service with Frontal Aviation in the shorter term and possibly the MiG-23 variable-geometry (swing-wing) fighter in the longer term. The Sukhoi and Mikoyan designs were under no circumstances in competition with each other; the T-10 being planned as a heavy fighter and the MiG-29 being planned as a light fighter capable of engaging its NATO (North Atlantic Treaty Organisation) opposite numbers, later typified by the General Dynamics (later Lockheed Martin) F-16 Fighting Falcon. In the event the T-10 design conducted its maiden flight on 20 May 1977; a redesign designated T-10S flying in 1981, this aircraft becoming the Su-27S which was designed to be capable of defeating the most modern western air superiority fighter aircraft then in service or development, typified by the F-15 Eagle.

Released in the 1980's, this US intelligence agency artist rendering of the Project 9 (MiG-29) apparently dates back to the late 1970's. The design is shown here in the capacity as an escort fighter for a Tupolev Tu-22M3 'Backfire' bomber. US DoD

The Project 9 metamorphosed into the MiG-29 which was of mainly aluminium-lithium alloy construction. Design features were optimised for high aerodynamic efficiency, including in the high alpha flight regime, embodying an integral aerodynamic layout optimised for high agility, featuring an integral wing-fuselage which effectively blended into a single structure. The blended high lift, low drag wing, which incorporated vortex generators, was designed for high lift, even when at high AoA (Angle of Attack) flight regimes. Much of the conventional flying controls were hydraulically actuated, but the flaps were computer controlled; the wing control surfaces consisting of the flaps inboard and ailerons on the outboard. Other features included twin all-moving vertical tail fins, rear horizontal tail planes and a side by side engine arrangement with significant spacing between them.

Early models featured an electro-mechanical FCS (Flight Control System) that, although being less advanced that the FBW (Fly By Wire) FCS's being installed in rival western designs, provided the basic MiG-29 with a degree of agility that exceeded those same western counterparts. That said, the MiG-29 was labour intensive to fly in comparison to its western analogues, this perhaps being its Achilles heel as pilot workload was intense by comparison to say the F-16, particularly during a combat scenario. It was possible for the pilot to override the g-limiter, but this would be an extreme last resort as it risked overstressing the aircraft and the pilot, in the latter case vastly increasing the risk of the pilot losing consciousness due to the excess forces of gravity.

With The Cold War at its height, the first grainy photographs of the MiG-29's encountered by NATO aircraft began to appear in the mid-1980's, this aircraft being shown armed with 2 x R-27R1 semi-active radar homing air to air missiles on the inboard wing stations and 4 x R-60 infrared homing air to air missiles on the intermediate and outer wing stations. Early MiG-29's were initially armed with the R-60 prior to deliveries of the highly agile R-73E. US DoD

This page: Among the first quality observations, certainly of ground operations, that western intelligence agencies got access to of the new Soviet light fighter aircraft came courtesy of photographs of a Soviet MiG-29 unit visit to Finland in 1986. US DoD

To power the Project 9 fighter, development of a new bypass turbofan engine commenced at Klimov (Sargisov) in 1971, variants of this engine, designated RD-33, going on to power all MiG-29 variants, two such units being the standard powerplant of all such variants prior to the introduction of the Unified Fighter Family in 2007.

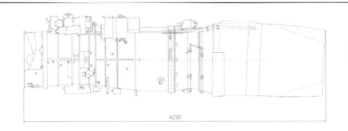

РД-33

основные технические характеристики		габаритные размеры, мм	
полный форсированный режим (H=0, M=0, σвх=1)		длина	4230
тяга, кгс	8300	ширина	1040
максимальный бесфорсажный режим (H=0, M=0, σвх=1)		высота	1160
тяга, кгс	5040	масса, кг	1218

Top: Russian language diagram of the Klimov RD-33 afterburning bypass turbofan engine. The thrust rating information translated to English corresponds to 8300 kgf thrust in afterburner, 5040 kgf thrust in dry military power. Engine dimensions and weight in English correspond to 4230 mm length, 1040 mm diameter, 1160 mm height and weight 1218 kg (conflicting Klimov documentation states weight as 1055 kg). Klimov **Above: The air intake of the MiG-29 was designed to allow adequate air to reach the engines even when the aircraft is flying at high AoA.** Author

Top: A Soviet/Russian MiG-29 fighter. Above: Post-Cold War, the MiG-29 would become the standard light fighter aircraft in service with the Russian Federation Air Force. RAC

The basic engine has a length of 4230 mm, diameter is 1040 mm and weight is 1055 kg. Available information shows the RD-33 to have a four stage fan and a nine stage pressure compressor. Lacking on early production examples, the RD-33 was eventually equipped with a FADEC (Full Authority Digital Engine Control) style system. The KSA-2/3 accessory gearbox is standard on RD-33 engines. The standard APU for the RD-33 is the GTDE-117 gas-turbine engine starter, development of which commenced in 1983, the same year that service deliveries of serial production MiG-29's commenced to the Soviet Air Forces. The GTDE-117, which weighs 42 kg, can be replaced by the VK-100, recommended for aircraft operating from air bases located at high altitudes, or the VK-150 when, as stated by Klimov, a "more robust starter" is required.

As stated by Klimov, the RD-33 has a maximum afterburning thrust of 8300 kgf for take-off, H=0, M=0, the MiG-29's excellent acceleration coming courtesy of the high thrust to weight ratio of the engines which exceeds the stated requirement of a ratio of 1:1, the combined maximum thrust of the two engines being in excess of the aircraft normal operational weight giving excess power for combat manoeuvring and acceleration, including power climbs. The climb rate for the MiG-29A was stated as 330 m/s, well in excess of the 270 m/s for the early F-16 models.

The 2 x 8300 kgf afterburning thrust of the Klimov RD-33 (values relate to the Series 2 engine) provides excess power for take-off with an adequate stores load and combat manoeuvring. RAC

The modular design of the engine enables parts to be quickly replaced at operational bases without the requirement for deep maintenance. Early engines proved unreliable with a time between overhaul of only around 350 hours. Introduction of the RD-33 Series 3 engine increased service life over earlier models.

The aircraft was designed for high operational turnaround featuring a number of design traits to ease maintenance with the ability to operate from short unpaved surfaces, one such design trait being the introduction of an advanced air intake design that incorporated a system procedure whereby the intake doors were closed during take-off and landing operations, air reaching the engine through louvres that are located on the upper and front wing. When the aircraft attains a certain airspeed the intakes open for normal operations. This system vastly reduces the risk of foreign object damage to the engines during take-off and landing.

The N019E radar system allowed even the earliest variants of the MiG-29 to guide the R-27R1 semi-active radar guided air to air missile, bestowing upon operators a radar guided medium range air to air capability, a capability lacking on the rival F-16 multirole fighter aircraft at the height of the Cold War throughout the 1980's. US DoD

In the primary air to air mission it was clear that the new lightweight fighter would have to counter the new generation of NATO low-level deep penetration strike aircraft such as the General Dynamics F-111 and the European Panavia Tornado (then known as the MRCA – Multi-Role Combat Aircraft). These advanced strike platforms were designed to penetrate heavily defended airspace at ultra-low-altitudes, necessitating that the Soviet lightweight fighter be equipped with a viable look down/shoot down capability to engage the aircraft in close proximity to the Earth's surface.

The integrated WCS (Weapon Control System), centred on the Phazotron NIIR N019E radar system (NATO reporting name 'Slot Back'), was a huge leap forward, capable of acquiring targets at long-range and low altitude, a capability lacking in previous generation Soviet systems. The WCS also included an OEPrNK-29E integrated optoelectronic sighting and navigation system which embodied an S-31E KOLS combined IRST (Infrared Search and Track) – UOMP (Ural Optical and Mechanical Plant) 13SM-1, referred to as an ORS (Optical Radar Station), and LR (Laser Range) finder, bestowing upon the aircraft a passive (radar-off) detection, tracking and engagement capability. The cockpit was dominated by the Windshield Projector – HUD (Heads up Display) that displayed a variety of flight information. A Shchel-3UM-1 basic HPS (Helmet Pointing System), the progenitor to the modern day HMTDS (Helmet Mounted Target Designation System), allowed the pilot to cue infrared guided air to air missiles to the target at high off-boresight angles, a capability lacking on NATO fighter aircraft for the next few decades.

The cockpit was typical of late 1970's cockpit technology with a plethora of analogue dials and standard flight controls. A voice alert system, known as Rita, gave voice warning if the aircraft was in flight modes likely to endanger the aircraft or if a threat such as an enemy missile was detected. The pilot was seated in a zero-zero capability ejection seat allowing emergency escape from the aircraft even when at zero altitude and zero airspeed.

The radar fire control system was complemented by an S-31E KOLS combined IRST/LR for operations against air and ground targets, the sensor element, which was part of the overall OEPrNK-29E system, being located forward of the windscreen offset to starboard. Author

For the flight development phase there were initially 11 Project 9 development aircraft designated 9-01 to 9-11, the first of which conducted its maiden flight on 6 October 1977. The aircraft underwent early flight testing at Ramenskoye, being observed there by a US spy satellite in November 1977, the design being allocated the NATO reporting name RAM-L as it was the eleventh experimental aircraft observed at the site (the letter I was apparently not used in the RAM reporting sequence).

The development aircraft were followed by eight MiG-29 pre-production aircraft designated 9-12 to 9-19, these aircraft being allocated to Frontal Aviation in 1983 for operational evaluation. Series production commenced in 1982, the first such aircraft being delivered to Kubinka air base during 1983, acceptance testing of the MiG-29A being completed in 1984, clearing the way for deliveries to operational units that same year.

Following delivery of around 100 airframes series aircraft production aircraft were modified by deletion of the ventral fins that had been introduced to the development aircraft following early flight testing. There were host of minor design changes introduced as production ramped up, including the introduction of rudders with extended chord, such designs being introduced to some surviving early examples by retrofit.

The MiG-29UB operational conversion trainer variant retained much of the operational capability of the single-seat aircraft, although the lack of provision for an on-board radar had the negative effect that it could not operate with the R-27R1 semi-active radar homing medium range air to air missile. RAC

When it entered service towards the mid-1980's, the basic MiG-29A, which was allocated the NATO reporting name 'Fulcrum' (later 'Fulcrum' A), was primarily intended as an air combat fighter for operations over the battlefields of the Central Front in Europe in the event that the Cold War turned hot. The aircraft did, however, have a secondary air to ground capability using a variety of unguided munitions, particularly rockets. Primary air to air armament was the R-27R1 SARH (Semi-Active Radar Homing) or R-27T1 passive IR (Infrared) homing medium range air to air missiles with a secondary armament of highly agile R-73E IR homing short-range air to air missiles. The tertiary air to air armament consisted of the internal Gsh-301 cannon housed in the port side forward fuselage/wing join with 150 rounds of ammunition, this latter weapon also being available for the secondary ground attack role.

In the 1980's, the MiG-29 had many performance advantages over the NATO F-16, particularly in such areas as speed, climb rate and manoeuvrability, particularly in the high AoA flight regime. The N019E radar system allowed the aircraft to employ R-27R1 radar guided medium range air to air missiles, a capability that was lacking on most F-16 variants until the advent of the AIM-120A AMRAAM in the early 1990's.

This MiG-29UB was operated from the Sokol Aircraft Production Plant. Sokol

When the MiG-29 appeared at Farnborough in September 1988, it introduced western observers to the world of Soviet (later Russian) high AoA agility flight, an area where Russia has retained its lead in the 21st century. Such manoeuvers were not just for show however. For example, the Bell manoeuvre, first performed on a MiG-

29 by test pilot Anatoly Kvochur, had a potential air combat application in that that it can cause a radar to break lock, be it an airborne radar in a fighter aircraft or air to air missile or a ground based radar tracking or targeting the subject aircraft. In regards to the ground based radar, the control tower at Farnborough apparently lost its screen blip for the MiG-29 when it performed the Bell manoeuvre in 1988.

While advanced MiG-29 derivatives currently represent the brand at trade shows the World over, the first generation aircraft is still represented at many events, often in the shape of the Russian Federation Air Force Swifts aerobatic display team. Like the MiG-29, the Swifts formation dates back to the Soviet era, 6 May 1991, when the team made their display debut in their white and blue livery with red and black Swifts on the air intakes.

A Russian MiG-29UB at the Canadian airbase at Abbotsford, Canada, in the early 1990's. US DoD

A two-seat operational conversion trainer variant of the MiG-29 was designed with the in house designation of 9-51 and the service designation MiG-29UB (NATO reporting name 'Fulcrum' B). This variant, which entered serial production in 1985, retained much of the operational capability of the single-seat aircraft, although lack of provision for an on-board radar meant that the aircraft could not guide the primary air to air armament of R-27R1 semi-active radar guided missiles. The aircraft could, however, operate with the R-27T1 and R-73E infrared guided air to air missiles, and simulation modes were included in the electronics suite to allow training for use of radar guided missiles. The number of MiG-29UB built was relatively small, in comparison to the numbers of single-seat aircraft.

Top: In the 1980's the Soviet Air Forces received a number of MiG-29S apparently equipped for a tactical nuclear strike role. This variant was easily distinguishable from the basic MiG-29A due to its distinctive humped spine housing electronic countermeasures equipment, some aircraft later being equipped with a fixed in-flight refueling probe located on the port side forward fuselage. Above: The first generation MiG-29M was developed in the late 1980's/early 1990' as a radically redesigned multirole variant introducing a number of airframe modifications and advanced (for the time) avionics and fire control system centred on the first generation N010 Zhuk radar. One of the most notable airframe modifications was deletion of the MiG-29's characteristic louvres on the upper wing fuselage join. RAC

A MiG-29SE demonstrates the type's air to air refuelling capability over a frozen landscape in the grip of a Russian winter. RAC

It is unclear how many Russian MiG-29's have been brought up to equivalent MiG-29SE standard, the variant initially being introduced for the export market by building on the MiG-29S, 9-13S, which first flew in 1984, an undisclosed number of 'S' models being built for the Soviet Union, this variant, which was allocated the NATO reporting name 'Fulcrum' C, featuring a bulged spine housing ECM (Electronic Counter Measures) equipment, some appearing with a fixed, non-retractable, in-flight refueling probe attached to the port side forward fuselage. The 'S' variant was apparently designed to be able to carry a single tactical nuclear weapon, although such a role would have been discontinued some years ago.

Most export deliveries from the mid-1990's onwards (including the MiG-29N for Malaysia which is a derivative of the MiG-29SE, 9-13SE, equipped with a retractable in-flight refueling probe on the port side forward fuselage) were to MiG-29SE standard, featuring enhancements to the radar, now designated N019ME, with incorporation of a new computer, increased internal fuel capacity and provision for a retractable in-flight refueling probe that replaced the fixed probe introduced on the MiG-29S. The MiG-29SE, however, lacked the bulged spine of the MiG-29S.

Armaments options for the MiG-29SE were increased with the addition of the enhanced capability R-27ER1 and R-27ET1 and the active radar guided RVV-AE, a maximum of two R-27 or six RVV-AE or six R-73E could be carried, or, of course, a mix of the various missile types. The number of external stores stations, at six, remained the same as the MiG-29Vers.B (this variant is also known as the MiG-29B, basically the export variant of the MiG-29A). Overall stores load was increased to 4500 kg and the aircraft could operate with three external fuel tanks – one on each of the inboard wing stations and one on the centre station – these being of some 1150 litre capacity (The MiG-29 Vers.B could carry only a single external fuel tank on operations, but could apparently carry three such tanks on a ferry mission) increasing the MiG-29SE range to 2900 km. Range values without external fuel tanks stood at 1500 km for the MiG-29 Vers.B and MiG-29SE, the MiG-29UB having a slight degradation at 1450 km. Range values with a single external fuel tank stood at 2100 km for the MiG-29 Vers.B and MiG-29SE and 2000 km for the MiG-29UB.

The standard MiG-29 single seat fighter was 17.32 m in length (MiG-29 Vers.B), wing span was 11.36 m and height was 4.73 m. Overall dimensions of the MiG-29UB were the same except in regards to length, which was increased to 17.42 m. Overall dimensions of the MiG-29SE remained the same as the earlier single-seat variants, but standard take-off weight was increased from 14900 kg of the MiG-29Vers.B to 15300 kg on the MiG-29SE and maximum take-off weight was increased from 18000 kg in the MiG-29Vers.B to 20000 kg in the MiG-29SE.

This aircraft, Blue 506, was displayed as a MiG-29SM at Farnborough in September 1996. The aircraft lacked an in-flight refueling probe, provision of which would have been available for service aircraft. Author

Overall kinetic performance remained more or less the same with maximum speed of the MiG-29Vers.B and MiG-29SE stated as 1500 km/h at sea level and 2400 km/h at altitude, with a maximum Mach number of 2.25. Ceiling was reduced from 18000 m for the MiG-29Vers.B to 17750 m in the MiG-29SE, both variants, along with the MiG-29UB, being powered by the RD-33 Series 2(3) engines.

The MiG-29SD designation referred to MiG-29's that were equipped with NATO and ICAO standard IFF (Identification Friend or Foe) and navigation equipment and a host of minor changes, this variant being aimed at Eastern European former Warsaw Pact countries having joined, or looking to join NATO, as well as Germany which had inherited East German MiG-29's on unification on 3 October 1990.

There were of course other variants, a whole family appearing in service or development form, including the original 1980's MiG-29K naval multi-role fighter and MiG-29M advanced (for the time) land based fighter, both of which eventually fell by the wayside. The demise of the original MiG-29K/M programs, however did not close the door on advanced multirole variants of the first generation MiG-29 airframe, a number of such variants emerging, commencing with the MiG-29SM in the mid-1990's leading to the MiG-29SMT which appeared in the late 1990's and was developed for service through the first few years of the 21st century.

The MiG-29SMT demonstrator, Blue 917, lands following a display at Farnborough in September 1998. Author

It would be a fair assessment to state that the MiG-29SM, 9-13SM, upgrade program was the straightening of the road that led to the MiG-29SMT multi-role variant. The SM variant incorporated enhancements to the fire control and avionics with a MIL STD 1553B data bus as standard. To the N019ME radar was added an independent radar channel centred on an MKV-04 computer. Other upgrades to the optical electronic fire control and data control systems included provision for a single MFD-54 MFCDS (Multi-Function Colour Display Screen), enhancements to the weapon management control system to facilitate the use of advanced precision strike weapons in addition to the R-27ER1, R-27ET1 and RVV-AE air to air missiles; six of the latter type could be carried. A multifunctional computer was added to the navigation suite, along with a GPS (Global Positioning System) receiver system and communications was enhanced by incorporation of an additional radio-station. The ECM protection could be increased courtesy of a podded system. Range figures were the same as those of the MiG-29SE when operating with or without external fuel tanks, but this could be increased to 5000 km by the use of in-flight refueling on the MiG-29SM or a MiG-29SE so equipped.

MiG-29SMT. RAC

The MiG-29SMT incorporated a modern fire control system in the shape of the Phazotron NIIR Zhuk-ME, this variant being offered as new build and as upgrades to existing first generation MiG-29 airframes. India selected a variation of the SMT for its MiG-29UPG upgrade of first generation MiG-29's and Russia received 28 MiG-29SMT and 6 upgraded MiG-29UB (the two-seat operational conversion trainer variant of the SMT was simply designated the Upgraded UB) originally ordered and then cancelled by Algeria. Yemen also received MiG-29SMT's and a number of Peru's MiG-29 fleet was upgraded to SMT standard, this variant also being operated by Eritrea and, in 2016, remains in production to fill an order for 16 additional aircraft for the Russian Federation Air Force.

In excess of 1600 MiG-29's were produced for the domestic Soviet and later Russian market and export; the aircraft being operated at one time or another by no less than 25 countries, among which included customers from the CIS (Commonwealth of Independent States), East European, Latin American, African, Middle East, Far East and the Indian sub-continent.

With the dissolution of the Soviet Union on Christmas Day 1991, some 800/900+ MiG-29's were in domestic service. Around 450/500 MiG-29's would remain in service in the new Russia while some 350 or so would be divided up between a number of former Soviet Republics, some surplus airframes finding their way to export customers. In early 2016, there are still several hundred first generation MiG-29's in Russian Federation service, and, while the serviceability of many of these have been questioned, the type still forms a significant element of Russia's combat aircraft fleet, although its importance will fade as the Russian Federation Air Force continues its modernisation drive with the introduction of several new types, including modern MiG-29SMT and, assuming the anticipated order is finalised, MiG-35/D to its inventory.

2

THE UNIFIED FIGHTER FAMILY

The original MiG-29K and MiG-29M programs dating back to the 1980's were aimed at fielding advanced (for the time) multirole variants of the MiG-29 for naval and terrestrial operations respectively. These programs, both of which fell into abeyance and then cancellation following the break-up of the Soviet Union in the early 1990's, despite their designations, share little more than a common ancestry with the 21st century MiG-29K/KUB and MiG-29M/M2 of the Unified Fighter Family.

The naval MiG-29K/KUB and its land based analogue, the MiG-29M/M2, which are basically land based derivatives of the MiG-29K/KUB, were launched in the early 21st century as members of a Unified Fighter family that would eventually include the MiG-35/D. The rationale behind the design of the Unified Fighter Family was the introduction of an number of improvements to address much of the deficiencies of the previous generation of MiG-29 fighters such as improved airframe construction with increased service life, improved flight performance, more advanced sensor/avionics suite (the open architecture avionics system is centered on MIL-STD-1553B standard bus's allowing easy incorporation of new systems of both domestic and foreign design) with complete data interchangeability, more accurate navigation, provision for more fuel, which, coupled with in-flight refuelling, increased range, and the ability for the aircraft to carry a heavier stores load with more external stores stations – eight on the MiG-29K/KUB and nine on the MiG-29M/M2. Overall combat efficiency would be increased along with aircraft serviceability and survivability, in the latter case a number of measures being implemented, these ranging from reduction in the radio electronic and infrared signatures as well as incorporation of an advanced electronic warfare/self-defence suite. An important feature for operators is the fact that the cost per flight hour has been reduced by an order of 2.5 times over that of first generation MiG-29 aircraft.

The MiG-29K/KUB is in service with the Russian and Indian Naval air arms as those nations main carrier borne combat aircraft. Development aircraft Blue 941 was painted in this attractive multi-tone blue livery. RAC

Compared to previous generation MiG-29's, the Unified Fighter Family introduced a redesigned, more efficient fuselage and wing. All members of the Unified Family sharing the same overall dimensions, length 17.3 m, height 4.4 m, some 0.33 m shorter than the first generation aircraft, and wing span 11.99 m; the wings being not only of increased span compared to the 11.36 m of the first generation aircraft, but also of increased area. Normal and maximum take-off weight is in the order of 3000 to 4000 kg higher than the MiG-29SE based on the first generation MiG-29 airframe. Increased load bearings allow 6500 kg of stores to be carried on nine external stations (eight on the MiG-29K/KUB); a multitude of radar and infrared guided air to air missiles for the air to air role and precision guided missiles and guided bombs can be employed in the air to ground and sea surface strike roles.

The Unified Fighter Family retained the highly efficient intake design, but, as was the case with the first generation MiG-29M, the characteristic upper intake mounted louvres of the first generation MiG-29 was omitted in the design of Unified Fighter Family, the risks of FOD (Foreign Object Damage) to the engines being reduced by the introduction of FOD avoidance grills that open and close in the intake, which feeds air to the engines. All members of the Unified Fighter Family were to be powered by a pair of RD-33MK afterburning turbofan engines featuring FADEC (Full Authority Digital Engine Control).

At the heart of the MiG-29K/KUB/M/M2 capabilities is the modern WCS (Weapon Control System) integrated through the RBKP PrNK-29 integrated fire control and navigation system. The Phazotron (Fazotron) NIIR Zhuk-ME radar is equipped with a slot-array antenna (FGM-129). This system can track up to 10 separate air targets, four of which can be simultaneously engaged with RVV-AE missiles. Integrated with the radar is the other major element of the weapon control system, the OLS (Optical Location Station) featuring an advanced multi-channel IRST/LR (Infrared Search and Track/Laser Range) finder which can be used to designate targets for missiles including such weapons as the R-73E short-range air to air missile and those equipped with passive warheads used in the anti-radar role.

From the programs genesis the Unified Fighter Family was designed around a common airframe, naval mission specific equipment such as an arrestor hook on the MiG-29K/KUB being the major external deference between the models. UAC

The Unified Fighter Family nose sections are manufactured by Sokol in Nizhny Novgorod before being transferred to MiG Corp No.2 facility where the remainder of the fuselage sub-units are manufactured and mated to the nose section before being transferred to MiG Corp. No.1 Production facility at Lukhovitsy near Moscow where the wings, empennage and a host of other structural components are manufactured. Aircraft final assembly then takes place at this facility.

In January 2004, India ordered sixteen MiG-29K/KUB fighters in a step towards modernising its naval air arm. The first batch was delivered in 2009 and the last aircraft were delivered in late 2011. In August 2010, assembly of the first of 29 additional MiG-29K/KUB's, ordered by India that March, commenced.

Russia became the second operator of the MiG-29K/KUB, twenty and four such aircraft respectively being ordered for the Russian Navy in February 2012, to supplement and eventually replace Sukhoi Su-33 naval fighters for operations from the Russian Navy's sole aircraft carrier. These aircraft being delivered through 2015.

The first of the MiG-29K/KUB aircraft conducted its maiden flight in January 2007 (stated in various documentation as 19 January –Klimov – and 20 January). A MiG-29KUB during its maiden flight (top) and landing (above). RAC

The MiG-29K/KUB are currently in service with the naval air arms of India (top) and Russia (above). RAC

The MiG-29M/M2 was developed as a land based variant of the MiG-29K/KUB, the major difference being in the elimination of naval specific equipment in the former. Top: The MiG-29M2, with MMRCA stenciling, is shown in formation with a first generation MiG-29M development aircraft; this latter aircraft being converted as the MiG-29OVT to flight test an Omni-directional thrust vectoring nozzle design. Above: The MiG-29M/M2 shared a common airframe with the MiG-29K/KUB. RAC

The first MiG-29M2 completed final assembly in late 2011 and flew on 24 December that year; being flown to MiG Corp's Zhukovsky facility three days later to commence flight testing there. The single-seat MiG-29M was flown by test pilot Stanislav Gorbunov on 3 February 2012. Production standard MiG-29M/M2's apparently entered assembly at RAC MiG's No.1 production facility at Lukhovitsy, Moscow, in 2013, although deliveries to the undisclosed Middle East customer have been postponed, if not outright cancelled.

The MiG-29M2 demonstrator was displayed at KADEX 2012 in Astana, the Capital of Kazakhstan in May 2012, marking the designs international debut; the aircraft being flown by test pilots Mikhail Belyayev and Stanislav Gorbunov. Gorbunov also flew with the First Deputy Commander of the Kazakh Air Force, Ulan Karbinov, in the rear seat as RAC tried, in vain, to interest Kazakhstan in the new fighter, Kazakhstan going on to order a small batch of four Sukhoi Su-30SM super-manoeuvrable multirole fighter aircraft which were delivered in 2015.

As part of the export drive RAC flew a MiG-29M2 from Russia to Batajnica air base in Serbia on 29 August 2012 to participate in the 100th anniversary of the Serbian Air Force air show. The aircraft was flown by RAC test pilot Stanislav Gorbunov and Alexander Pelikh. Serbia, although in dire need of modern combat aircraft to replace its obsolete combat aircraft force, is likely to be unable to fund any substantial order in the foreseeable future.

As the MiG-35/D began to take centre stage for RAC's export drive, the MiG-29M/M2 demonstrators, 741 and 747 respectively, were presented as MiG-35's at MAKS 2013. These aircraft assumed their true MiG-29M/M2 identities again for the MAKS 2015 event, MiG-29M2 747 taking part in the flying display while MiG-29M 741 was present in the static park where it was displayed with a plethora of advanced air launched weapons.

MiG-29K development aircraft 941 refuels from an Ilyushin Il-76 tanker aircraft. RAC

MiG-29M2, Blue 747, in formation with a restored World War 2 era MiG-3 piston engine fighter (top) and during ground operations (bottom). RAC

3

MiG-35/D DESIGN AND EVOLUTION

Clearly an advanced evolution of the MiG-29K/KUB/M/M2 Unified Fighter Family, which are themselves derived from the original MiG-29 dating back to the 1970's, the MiG-35, which shares many of the formers design traits, is a 4th++ generation multirole combat aircraft designed as a MiG-29 replacement for the 21st century.

More or less structurally identical to the other members of the Unified Fighter Family from which it evolved, the MiG-35/D features a number of improvements that led to it being characterised as a 4th++ generation multirole combat aircraft incorporating a number of 5th generation systems, whereas its forebears were characterised as 4th+ generation multirole combat aircraft. The MiG-29M/M2 was itself almost structurally identical to the MiG-29K/KUB; removal of the latter's arrestor hook being the major structural change. The high-lift devices on the wing of the MiG-29K were retained in the other members of the Unified Fighter Family, as was the wing panel design. As with the other members of the Unified Fighter Family, the MiG-35/D features a retractable in-flight refueling capability and the ability to be utilised as an ersatz air tanker whereby it can refuel other aircraft in-flight. The increased corrosion protection for the airframe that was introduced with the MiG-29K/KUB was retained in the MiG-29M/M2 and MiG-35/D; in the terrestrial based MiG-29M/M2 and MiG-35/D this allows these aircraft to operate more efficiently in tropical climates.

While there is no pretense at the aircraft being a 5th generation 'stealth' design in the mould of the US Lockheed Martin F-22 Raptor or the Sukhoi T-50 PAK FA, a reduction in the 4th generation level radar signature was achieved in the MiG-29K/KUB through such measures as achieving a smoother outer finish and applying 'special' outer coatings, this being carried over to the MiG-35/D, as were measures taken to reduce infrared signature.

The MiG-35/D is, in 2016, the pinnacle of the evolution of the Project 9 (MiG-29) dating back to the 1970's. Although radically redesigned, the Unified Fighter Family show clear design lineage from the basic MiG-29A of 1977. RAC

Basic dimensions, at a length of 17.3 m, wing span 11.99 m and height 4.4 m, are as the figures for the MiG-29K/KUB/M/M2. No weight figures have been released by RAC or UAC for the MiG-35/D, which would be expected to be closer to those of the MiG-29M/M2 values than those values for the MiG-29K/KUB. Normal take-off weight figures for the MiG-29K/KUB are given as 18500 kg and 18650 kg respectively, those for the MiG-29M/M2 being somewhat lower at 17500 kg and 17800 kg respectively. Maximum take-off weight figures for the MiG-29K/KUB are given as 24500 kg for both variants. No figures have been released by RAC or UAC for the MiG-29M/M2 or the MiG-35/D, but Rosoboronexport documentations states values of 23500 kg for the MiG-35/D. In all variants of the Unified Fighter Family the weight figures are well in excess of the respective values of 15300 kg and 20000 kg for normal take-off and maximum take-off weight of the MiG-29SE development of the first generation MiG-29 airframe.

As with the MiG-29M/M2, the MiG-35/D benefits from the strengthened undercarriage designed for the MiG-29K/KUB, allowing the higher operating weights to be achieved. Increased load bearings allow stores to be carried on nine external stations; a multitude of precision guided stand-off missiles and guided bombs can be employed in the air to ground and sea surface strike roles.

The MiG-35/D enhancements over the MiG-29M/M2 are mainly internal, including integration of fifth generation information sighting systems into the overall sensor/avionics suite. Aircraft survivability is enhanced courtesy of the incorporation of an enhanced airborne integrated defense system.

Three-view general arrangement drawing of the MiG-35/D. Both the single-seat MiG-35 and the two-seat MiG-35D, as is the case with other members of the Unified Fighter Family, retained a common fuselage, the MiG-35 having an additional fuel tank in place of the MiG-35D's rear cockpit equipment. RAC

Graphics detailing the MiG-35/D's improved airframe design. UAC

The multitude of roles set out for the MiG-35/D, air superiority (for which the manufacturer states the aircraft can effectively combat fifth generation fighter aircraft), include close and medium range air to air combat, precision strike against ground targets, anti-ship strike and a reconnaissance capability courtesy of the optical-electronic and radio-technical (radar) equipment. In the air to air role the MiG-35/D can participate in group actions, including air control operations whereby the aircraft would take control of groups of other fighter aircraft, handing off targeting information as required via a datalink system. The advanced infrared and radar guided air to air missiles allow the aircraft to engage airborne targets at low, medium and high altitudes from medium to close range, the internal Gsh-301 30 mm cannon capable of being employed in the air to air and air to surface roles.

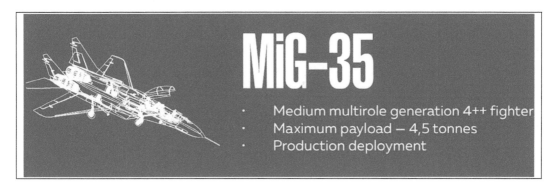

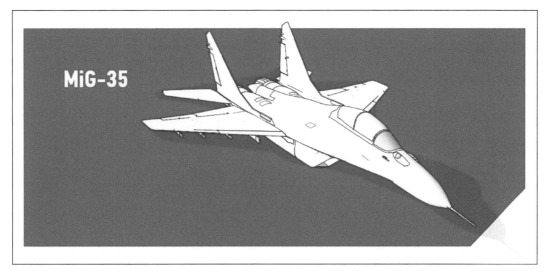

Ghosted view (top) and semi-frontal/lateral view (above) graphics of the MiG-35/D. UAC

The advanced FBW (Fly By Wire) FCS (Flight Control System) ensures the MiG-35/D can maintain excellent stability and control during many automatic and manual flight profiles, including the designs much lauded super-manoeuvrability, even in extreme high alpha manoeuvers.

Details of the FCS system employed by the MiG-35/D remain hazy, but it is assumed that this system, referred to as the KSU-961, is a variation of the MKPK Avionica KSU-941 Integrated Flight Control System developed for the MiG-29K/KUB. The manufacturer description of this system reads, "The digital redundant integrated flight control system... accomplishes tasks of fly-by-wire and automatic control systems, as well as implements the following functions:

- Digital control of servo units
- Automatic limitation of angle of attack and acceleration during manual and automatic control
- Automatic control of segmented wing leading-edges
- Automatic control of flaps
- Reduction of wing and maneuvering loads
- Automatic compensation of aerodynamic loads during leading-edges, brake flaps, flaps and aileron extension
- Aircraft stability and controllability during in-flight refueling
- Automatic engine thrust control including in the case of shutdowns
- Automatic withdrawal of the aircraft from a dangerous low altitude pre-selected by a pilot.

KSU-941 has built-in check aids, which provide:
- KSU-941 serviceability pre-flight check
- KSU-941 operating maintenance without ground-check equipment
- KSU-941 automatic adjustment without ground-check equipment.

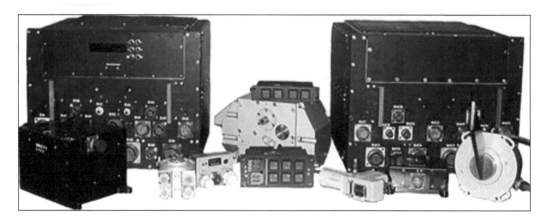

The MiG-35/D FBW FCS is loosely referred to as the KSU-961 unit, which is apparently a derivative of the KSU-941 (above) installed in the MiG-29K/KUB.

As briefly noted in the previous chapter the resurgence of advanced MiG-29 derivatives, commencing with the MiG-29K/KUB, led to development of a modernised, more powerful variant of the Klimov RD-33 engine to power the Unified Fighter Family. This new engine variant emerged as the RD-33MK (Sea Wasp) which was first flown on a MiG-29K/KUB in January 2007.

While retaining the RD-33's good qualities such as the designers stated "unrestricted flight control and high stability against ambient disturbances", the RD-33MK introduced a number of improvements such as a 7% higher thrust rating; take-off thrust now standing at 9000 kgf, enhancing the MiG-29K/KUB's carrier take-off capabilities, particularly in hot climates, a key requirement for India, the MiG-29K/KUB launch customer. The higher thrust of the RD-33MK, which is, according to Klimov, attributed to the incorporation of "cooled blades made of modern materials including composites", allows the MiG-29K/KUB to perform unassisted take-offs from the decks of aircraft carriers. For the ground based MiG-29M/M2 and MiG-35/D, the higher thrust ratings allow the aircraft to operate more efficiently at higher operating weights and, as with the MiG-29K/KUB, provide extra power for combat manoeuvring.

The KSA-2/3 accessory gearbox of the standard RD-33 was replaced in the RD-33MK with a KSA-33M, a new generation accessory which, according to Klimov documentation, consists of "two kinematically independent gearboxes with a separate drive for each engine." Its duel system backup improves safety and improves survivability. The accessory gearbox provides for the operation of the aircraft electric and hydraulic systems, both on the ground and in the air. Other features of the powerplant include a VK-100 turbine starter and a BARK-42 automatic control and monitoring unit; this latter system entering production in 2008. The engine also features an IDS (Information and Diagnostics System).

Despite the higher power ratings, a key requirement for the RD-33MK was increased service life over the previous generation engine, which for the RD-33MK stands at 4,000 hours. The new engine infrared and optical signatures were reduced over its forebear, contributing to the reduction in the overall optical and infrared signature of the Unified Fighter Family.

Development of the RD-33MK commenced in 2001. From bench testing to its first flight in a MiG-29K/KUB development aircraft in January 2007, the RD-33MK underwent the full spectrum of testing, official Russian Federation government tests being completed on 18 December 2012, clearing the engine for operational use.

While RD-33 Series 2 engines were manufactured by Baranov OMO Enterprise in Omsk, the RD-33MK, like the RD-33 Series 3 engines produced for the MiG-29SMT, are manufactured by Moscow based Chernyshev Machine-Building Enterprise.

RD-33MK mock-up. RAC

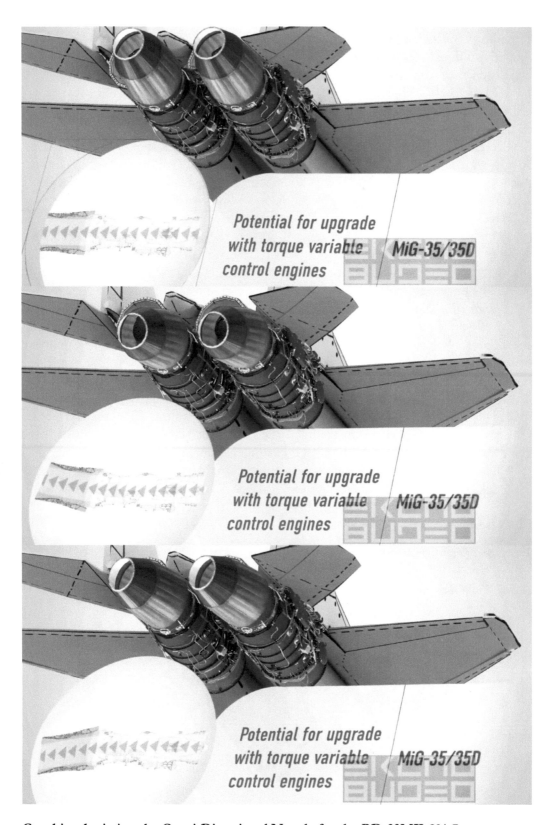

Graphics depicting the Omni-Directional Nozzle for the RD-33MK. UAC

Klimov ODN (Omni-Directional Nozzle) system. Klimov

As demonstrated with the first public display routines in the late 1980's, the basic MiG-29 design was endowed with excellent maneuvering capabilities that, for the most part, exceeded those of its western rivals, particularly in the low-speed high alpha flight regime, design traits that have been carried over to the Unified Fighter Family. However, in a drive to increase the maneuvering capabilities further, so as to rival the super-manoeuvrability of the Sukhoi Su-30MKI series and later the Su-35S, the designers embarked upon a program to develop a viable thrust vector control capability for the engine nozzles of the RD-33 and the RD-33MK.

For the flight test elements of the program one of the original 1980/1990's MiG-29M development aircraft was modified to accept an ODN (Omni-Directional Nozzle) system in place of the standard engine nozzles for its RD-33 Series 2 engines. Klimov states that the ODN "is based on the universal KLITV (Klimov Thrust Vector) technology" and "can be installed on Russian and foreign turbojet (turbofan) engines of any design." UAC graphics show the MiG-35/D equipped with ODN, which would, as stated by Klimov, increase combat efficiency by 12-15%. As well as enhancing aircraft manoeuvrability, particularly in the slow-speed post stall flight regime, incorporation of thrust vector control enhances the aircraft performance in other areas such as take-off and landing.

The Klimov description of the ODN reads "The axisymmetric exhaust unit system with a turning supersonic part of the jet nozzle provides for omnidirectional (360°) deflection of the thrust vector. A TVN-equipped engine of a combat aircraft notably improves its maneuverability at subsonic speeds and supercritical angles of attack. While improving the performance of aircraft, TVN nozzles also enhance safety during take-off and landing as well as under challenging conditions."

Page 36-38: The ODN test bed was the first generation MiG-29M development aircraft No.156, which was designated MiG-29OVT after conversion, which included fitting ODN to the RD-33 Series 2 engines. Although associated with development of the Unified Fighter Family, the MiG-29OVT was intended to prove the ODN capability for all versions of the MiG-29/35. RAC

Klimov documentation shows that the "Nozzle control is not restricted in any flight mode, including the afterburning mode" and that the "thrust vector deflection angle" can be + 15° in any direction, the speed of deflection being 60°/second.

The Klimov ODN was publically unveiled at the MAX-98 exhibition. A first generation MiG-29M, No.156, was converted as the ODN test bed with the designation MiG-29OVT, this aircraft being exhibited for the first time in this capacity at the MAX air show in 2005. The test program showed that a MiG-29 derived aircraft equipped with the ODN for the RD-33 or RD-33MK engines can achieve extraordinary levels of manoeuvrability, particularly in the low-speed high alpha flight regime. As well as the RD-33/RD-33MK, the ODN can be adapted for compatibility with other in-service or projected combat aircraft engines.

The MiG-35/D is equipped with an integrated fire control and navigation system centred on the PrNK-35 which is derived from the PrNK-29KR/KUBR (above) developed for the MiG-29KR/KUBR in Russian naval aviation service. RPKB

The MiG-35/D fire control and avionics navigation systems are integrated through what is loosely termed the PrNK-35 (this designation has not been confirmed by the manufacturer), which is a variation of the PrNK-29KR/KUBR integrated fire control and navigation system installed in the MiG-29K/KR/KUB/KUBR. As stated by RPKB, this system, in conjunction with other avionics systems, "provides accurate weapons delivery and precise navigation." The system comprises a computing system, the weapon control system, data control system and navigation system. The central digital computing system is designed to run in excess of ten high level tasking's simultaneously.

One of the major elements of the data control system is the wide-angle HUD (Heads up Display), which dominates the forward view outside the cockpit. The type of HUD, upon which is superimposed various data such as flight, targeting, fuel and weapon status, will depend on customer requirements, domestic aircraft that may be ordered for the Russian Federation Air Force possibly being equipped with a variation of the IKSH-1M HUD collimator installed on the Su-35S, a variation of which also equips the Su-30SM 'super-manoeuvrable multirole fighter aircraft in Russian service. Other elements of the data control system include the control panel, three colour MFDS (Multi-Function Display Screens) in the front cockpit, power supply and an interface system. In the two-crew MiG-35D, additional elements of the data control system in the rear cockpit includes four colour MFDS and additional instrumentation for navigation. The two-seat aircraft is also equipped with instrumentation and controls for a second pilot or instructor, although it is unclear if this equipment is an option or standard. The HOTAS (Hands on Throttle and Stick) concept is incorporated, certainly in the front cockpit, but also as an option in the rear cockpit, many flight and targeting functions able to be conducted without letting go of the stick control stick.

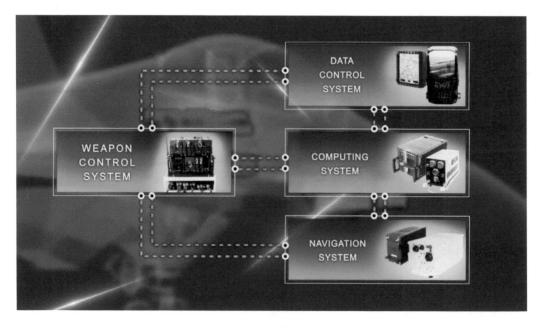

The PrNK-35, like the PrNK-29KR/KUBR, integrates the weapon control system, data control system, computing system and the navigation system. RPKB

The most significant enhancement in the MiG-35/D is the incorporation of the Zhuk-AE active-phased-array radar which bestows a major leap in capability over its forebear, the Zhuk-ME equipping the MiG-29K/KUB and MiG-29M/M2 (slot-array FGM-129) and MiG-29SMT and derivatives (slot-array FGM-229). Enhancements include a wider range of operating frequencies, an increase in the amount of airborne and ground targets that can be detected, tracked and engaged simultaneously and increased range at which targets can be detected. Image resolution in the surface mapping mode is increased and the system features increased resistance to jamming.

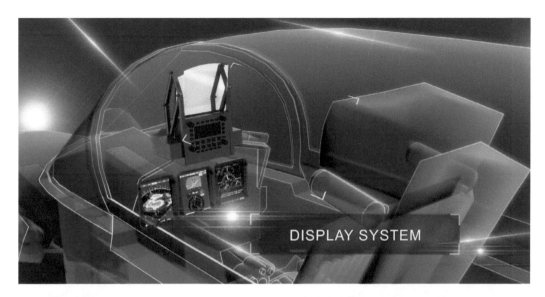

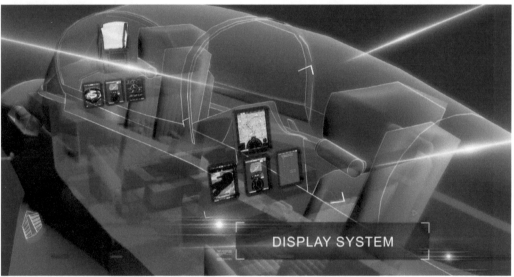

The main elements of the data control system in the MiG-35 (top) and MiG-35/D (above). RPKB

In the air to air role the Zhuk-AE can track 30 targets and engage six simultaneously, a significant advance on the 10 and 4 respectively for the Zhuk-ME. No official figures for target detection ranges have been released, but these are stated to be in excess of those achieved by the Zhuk-ME, which is 130 km for an airborne target moving forward in free space, 50 km for an airborne target moving in pursuit in free space, 120 km for an airborne target moving forward against the Earth's background and 40 km for an airborne target moving in pursuit against the Earth's background. Zhuk-ME detection ranges for surface targets are given as 200 km for a destroyer size target, 80 km against a missile boat size target, 120 km against a railway bridge and 30 km against a group of moving tanks.

Phazotron NIIR embarked upon development of an AESA (Active Electronically Scanned Array) for the Zhuk radar, referred to as the APAR (Active Phased Array Radar), in the middle of the first decade of the 21st century. A demonstrator radar, designated FGA-29, with a 500 mm diameter AESA, underwent bench testing in 2006. This radar was then installed on the MiG-35D demonstrator, Blue 154, before the aircraft was displayed at Aero India in Bangalore in 2007.

MiG-35D, side code 967, conducted flight trials with a Zhuk AESA in April 2010, with Russian and Indian Air Force pilots flying the aircraft during the test phase, which included a number of missile launches.

The Zhuk-AE (FGA-35), intended for production standard MiG-35/D fighters, is equipped with a 688 mm diameter AESA antenna, with the number of available T/R (Transmit/Receive) modules, at just over 1000, being almost doubled compared to the number incorporated on the FGA-29.

Although the Zhuk-AE (FGA-35) is the standard specified for the MiG-35/D, Phazotron is developing a completely new AESA which, under current planning, is to be equipped with new T/R modules developed by NIIP Semiconductor Instrument Research Institute located in Tomsk. This system, it is assumed, is intended for integration on the MiG-35/D and other advanced fighter aircraft.

Previous page: The MiG-35/D demonstrator, Blue 154, with its FGA-29 AESA exposed. Above: The FGA-29 was the first version of the Zhuk-AE to be installed in the MiG-35D demonstrator. Phazotron NIIR

Zhuk AE (FGA-35) – Data furnished by Phazotron NIIR

- Target detection with the measurement of angular coordinates, range, velocity in the free space - look-up mode, on the background of the earth (the sea) - look down mode
- Single-target track
- Support the tracking of 30 targets while maintaining the review of space (track while scan mode) and at the same time attack 6 targets
- Capture and maintenance of visually apparent purpose in the conduct of passing maneuver battlefield
- Close maneuvering combat modes (Vertical, HUD field of view, sighting, boresight)
- Detection and attack of helicopters, including those in 'hovering' mode
- Detection of the class, the type and size of targets and the number of targets in the group
- 'Air-to-surface'
- Terrain mapping, real beam narrowing of the Doppler beam with focused synthetic aperture antenna. Upscaling the freezing card
- Air to ground ranging
- Sea surface search
- Overview of the sea surface
- Detection of stationary and moving ground (sea) targets
- simultaneous track of 2 stationary or moving ground-sea-surface targets
- Measurement of host aircraft speed
- Data support to aid low-altitude flight operation
- Simultaneous operation modes 'air-to-air' and 'air-to-surface'

Additional features
- Measuring the distance to the ground
- Measure the speed of the carrier
- Information support for low-altitude flight
- The 'Meteo'

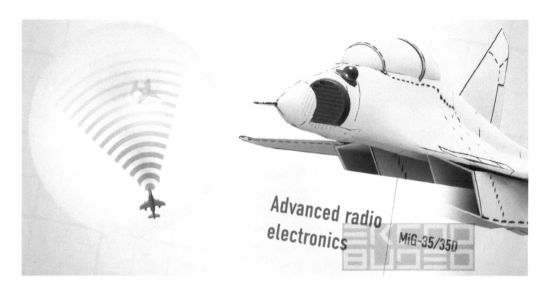

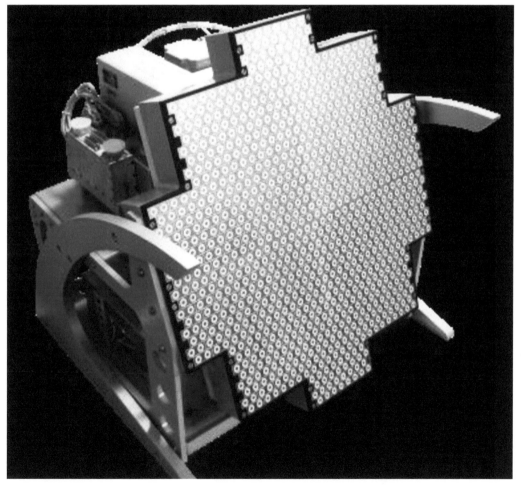

The technological advances made with the Zhuk-AE (FGA-35 above) correspond to a quantum leap in capability over the Zhuk-ME system installed in the MiG-29K/KUB/M/M2. UAC

Basic parameters of the Zhuk-AE (data furnished by Phazotron NIIR applies to the FGA-29):

Operating frequency	X-band
Antenna	AESA
Diameter	575 mm
Gain	35 dB
Angle movements	
Azimuth/elevation	+60°
Scan zones	±10°/±30°/±60°
Noise factor	3 dB
Pulse power	3400 W
Target detection range… in air to air modes	
Look up	
Head-on aspect	130 km
Tail on aspect	60 km
Look down	
Head-on aspect	120 km
Tail-on aspect	50 km
Target detection range in air to surface modes	
Destroyer	200 km
Missile boat	80 km
Railway bridge	120 km
Group of moving tanks	30 km
Azimuth and range resolutions	
Low resolution (R=80 km)	300x300
Medium resolution (R=60 km)	30x30
High resolution (R=20 km)	1x1
Parameters	
Mass	200 kg
Input power	
AC(AYA)	5
DC (kW)	1.0
Cooling	air & liquid
MTBF	500 h

The MiG-35 is equipped with the same JSC Scientific and Production Corporation Precision Instrumentation OLS-UE optical location station as the MiG-29K/KUB. RAC

Other elements of the weapons control system include the OLS (Optical Location Station), HMTDS (Helmet Mounted Target Designation System), HUD (noted as an element of the data control system), and the IFF (Identification Friend or Foe) interrogator. Manufacturer documentation shows the MiG-35/D to be equipped with the JSC SPC CPR (JSC Scientific and Production Corporation Precision Instrumentation Systems) OLS-UE Optical Location Station employed by the MiG-29K/KUB and MiG-29M/M2. The OLS-UE consists of an IRST (Infrared Search and Track) system that combines Infrared, TV (Television) and laser sighting systems with a LR (Laser Range) finder. A pod mounted IRST system can also be mounted on the fuselage underside. Employment of the OLS allows the aircraft to detect, track and engage targets passively without the need for radar, the emissions of which can betray the host aircraft own position. In addition, as has been the case with other combat aircraft, the OLS is one of the main-elements of the so called 'counter stealth' technology revolution that has quickly eroded the low-observable advantages of aircraft designed with low-observable technologies. For example, the PIRATE system installed on the Eurofighter Typhoon is stated to have detected Lockheed Martin F-22 air dominance fighters at ranges of around 50 km, there being no reason to believe that Russian designed systems would be any less capable.

JSC SPC CPR documentation shows that "structurally the OLS-UE consists of 4 blocks"; Block optical mechanical (bom); processing unit (BOI); the unit of processor (BDP) and the control unit drives (BUP). The system provides for "a review of the aircraft in the forward hemisphere airspace, land and water surfaces, Search, detection, capture, and auto tracking, determination of angular coordinates and range up to the air, ground and sea targets (LC, SC and NEC) in the mid-infrared (3... 5 m) and visible ranges, Laser illumination NC". The system is cooled by "air, natural convection and forced convection (air flow due to the side.)".

The OLS-UE provides the MiG-35/D with a passive detection, tracking and engagement capability, being one of the main 'counter stealth' systems designed to erode the advantages of aircraft designed for low radar signature. JSC SPC CPR

Information furnished by the development team indicates that OLS-UE provides for "airspace scanning in 'Air-to-air' mode; Aerial, ground and water surface target detection, locking-on and tracking; Ground surface scanning; Target image recognition; Target angular coordinates, range and angular linear velocity determination; TV, IR and TV+IR video and message output to the cockpit multifunctional displays; interaction with the aircraft target and guidance complex; Operation at full range of altitudes, ground and sky backgrounds, day and night time, visual meteorological conditions and jamming interference; Ground target illumination by laser emission; autonomous functioning and radio silence mode.".

JSC SPC CPR OLS-UE	
Scanning angular limits:	
Azimuth	±90°
Elevation	-15° to +60°
Airborne detection range against a Su-30 size target:	
In rear hemisphere of target	< 60 km
In front hemisphere of target	< 15 km
Range measurement	
Airborne target	< 15 km
Ground target	< 20 km
Instant field of view	10 x 7.5°
Dimensions 729 mm x 386 mm x 410 mm	
Mass	78 kg

The nose mounted OLS is augmented by the so called 'next generation optronics' system located on the starboard engine bay underside. RAC

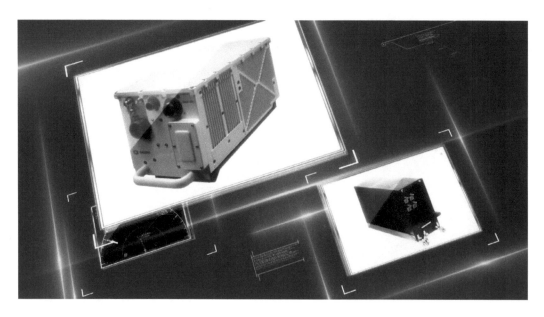

The navigation element of the PrNK-35 consists of the inertial navigation system, air data system and short-range navigation system. RPKB

The baseline navigation suite includes the inertial satellite navigation system, air data system and short-range navigation. Any Russian purchase of MiG-35/D fighters is expected to include incorporation of a BINS-SP-2 Strapdown Inertial Navigation System that does not rely on satellites to determine coordinates, accurate navigation being possible in the absence of such GPS (Global Positioning System) and offshore ground based navigation data. BINS can determine the exact location of a particular air vehicle, process data and then transfer flight and navigation data to a receiver. In short, states Kret, parent company of the system developer MIEA (Moscow Institute of Electromechanics and Automation), "BINS is able to determine the coordinates and parameters of an object in offline mode and without ground-based, naval, or satellite signals." BINS was in testing in 2015, several systems being involved in tests for the MoD of the Russian Federation.

As stated by RPKB, manufacturer of the PrNK system that integrates a number of the systems including navigation, automatic control can be utilised for "all flight legs, including approach to specified point at scheduled time for the following attack." RPKB continues, "The system provides low altitude flight and auto-landing by the use of satellite navigation system. The system is equipped for flights in civil airspace." In the MiG-29K, the navigation system includes a ship landing airborne radio system that is omitted from the MiG-35/D.

The MiG-35/D is apparently equipped with a Karat-B-35 flight data recorder consisting of SVR-23M1K video recorder unit and a Trenazh-29 weapon simulation system. It is unclear what stores management system will be installed in series production MiG-35/D aircraft, but, certainly for export aircraft, this will probably be supplied by Aviaavtomatika, the supplier of the SUO (Stores Management System) installed in the Indian MiG-29K/KUB – SUO-29K, MiG-29UPG upgrade for India – SUO-29KI and Yemen and Eritrean MiG-29SMT – SOU-30PK-29.

It can be inferred that the MiG-35/D is equipped with the BLP-3.5-1(2) Emergency Escape Logic Unit that is installed in the MiG-29K/KUB, or a derivative of that unit. This system, an element of the electrical emergency escape system, is, as stated by the manufacturer "intended to generate sequence of commands controlling operation of the airborne system actuating mechanisms and ejection seats in case of aircraft emergency escape."

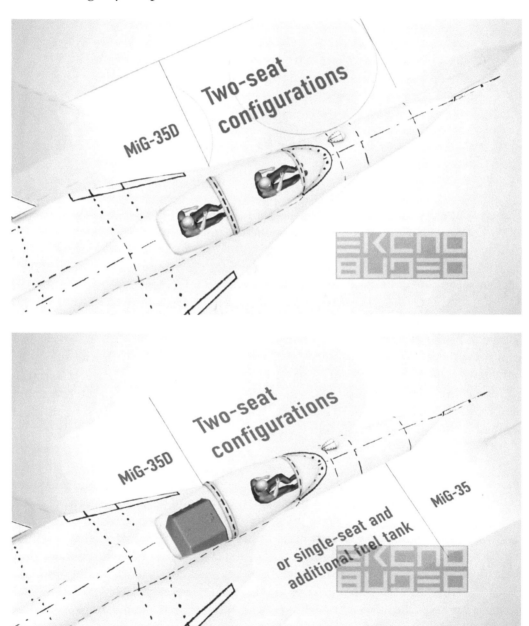

The MiG-35 is available in both two-seat, MiG-35D, (top) and single-seat, MiG-35, (above) configurations. In the single-seat aircraft free space of the second cockpit area can accommodate an additional fuel tank. UAC

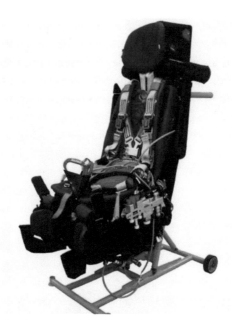

The crew of the various members of the Unified Fighter Family are accommodated on NPP Zvezda K-36D-3.5M zero-zero ejection seat. NPP Zvezda

The MiG-35/D crew is accommodated on NPP Zvezda K-36D-3.5M zero zero ejection seats (one in the MiG-35 and two in the MiG-35D) that are also installed in the MiG-29M/M2 and MiG-29K/KUB. This seat is a derivative of the K-36D-3.5 installed in a number of combat aircraft including all Sukhoi Su-30 variants.

The NPP Zvezda description of this seat reads, "The crewmember protection against the dynamic pressure G-loads at ejection is provided with the protection gear, windblast shield, forced restraint in the seat, seat stabilization as well as the selection of one of three operation modes for the emergency source depending on the suited pilot mass. At the aircraft speed exceeding 850 km/h, the MRM steady-state mode is adjusted by the automatics depending on the acceleration."

"After automatic separation of the pilot from the seat, the recovery parachute canopy is inflated providing the pilot's safe descent. A portable survival kit, which is separated from the seat together with the pilot, supports his/her vital functions after landing or water landing, makes the pilot search easier, and the... -1 life raft supports the pilot floatation on the surface of the water."

"The K-36D-3.5 ejection seat realizes the crewmember emergency escape within the range of equivalent airspeed (V_E) from 0 to 1300 km/h, at Mach number up to 2.5 and aircraft flight altitude from 0 to 20000 m, including takeoff, landing run and H=0, V=0 mode. The seat is used with the KKO-15 set of protective gear and oxygen equipment." The weight of the seat and survival kit is around 103 kg.

The Zvezda KC-129 oxygen system, according to manufacturer information, provides oxygen for the crew "when flying at altitudes up to 20 km. The source of the oxygen is an onboard oxygen installation BKDU-130, producing oxygen from the compressed air taken from the compressor of the aircraft engine." This means that there is no need for onboard oxygen cylinders, with the knock-on effect that there is no requirement to top up with oxygen before each flight which is not limited in duration due to lack of oxygen supplies. As well as the MiG-35/D the KC-129 system is also incorporated on the MiG-29K/KUB/M/M2 and MiG-29UPG as well as Sukhoi 4+/4++ generation fighter aircraft, the Su-30MKI/SM and Su-35S.

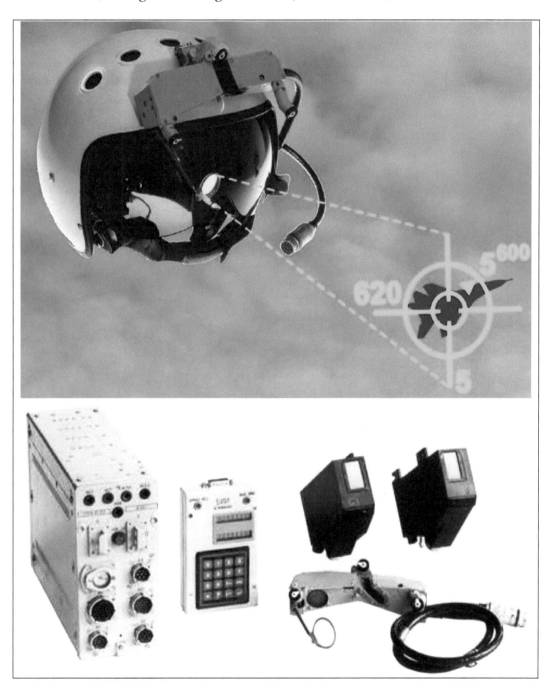

The baseline HMTDS for the MiG-35/D is apparently the SURA-M, export operators able to employ the SURA, SURA-K or foreign sources systems.

The baseline HMTDS (Helmet Mounted Target Designation System) specified for the MiG-35/D is apparently the SURA-M system that also equips the Su-30SM in Russian Federation Air Force service. The baseline unit for export aircraft will probably be the SURA, SURA-K or, alternatively, the improved SURA-I HMTDIS (Helmet Mounted Target Designation and Indication System). Potential export aircraft may be equipped with other systems such as the Thales TopSight specified for the MiG-29K/KUB in service with the Indian Navy.

The SURA-M and SURA can, according to manufacturer documentation, scan the airspace ±70° in azimuth and -35° to +65° in elevation with a designation accuracy (RMS error) of < 3 mrad. The entire system weighs 6 kg (SURA-M) and 10 kg (SURA), the helmet mounted element weighting 0.39 kg.

In simplified terms the HMTDS, which receives signal inputs from the various on-board systems, displays flight and targeting information on a visor on the pilot flight helmet. This data, which is displayed in symbolic and alphanumeric form, with various data types and volumes specified by individual operators, is projected onto a field of view of 6°x4° on the SURA-M.

The MiG-35/D is equipped with an extensive self-defense suite with various sensors located along the forward fuselage sides, the spine and the wingtips. RAC

The MiG-35/D is endowed with an advanced self-defence suite that, according to RAC, includes "radio electronic reconnaissance and electronic counter measures; optronic systems for detection of attacking missiles and laser emission; decoy dispensers to counteract the enemy in radar and infrared ranges." The aircraft will also incorporate sensors for UV (Ultra Violet) irradiation of attacking missiles.

One system specified for incorporation on the MiG-35/D is the Avtomatika Design Bureau L-150 ELINT (Electronic Intelligence) suite with antennas embedded in the aircraft wingtips and vertical tail planes. Other systems include an NIIPP laser illumination warning system with receivers located on the wingtips. A NIIPP missile warning receiver is located behind the cockpit on the top of the fuselage with another receiver located under the port side air intake. The JSC Kaluzhsky Scientific Research Radio-Technical Institute SAP-518 and KS-418 active ECM (Electronic Counter Measures) suite (the ECM suite can be carried internally or in podded systems) or a combination of both.

Antennas for the KNIRTI Radiotechnical Research Institute ESM (Electronic Sensor Measures) systems are located in in the LERX's and aircraft tail section. Another antenna can be found in an attachment located under the port wing panel.

Series production aircraft will be equipped with an active RF (Radio Frequency) jammer system although the type of system will depend on the customer requirements. One of the most modern active jammer developed in Russia is the President-S active RF jammer which is used to protect the host aircraft radar guided air to air and surface to air missiles and other radar guided air defence systems. The system effectively jams the tracking/homing radar of the attacking missile at multiple stages of the engagement – detection, tracking and attack.

The system, initial development of which was completed in 2015, can be carried on various platforms, including tactical combat aircraft. It uses a host of digital signal processing and countermeasures techniques DRFM (Digital Radio Frequency Memory). The system is capable of protecting the host aircraft by jamming hostile radar, even in complex threat environments that involve radar systems such as targeting missile radar or tracking airborne/surface radar.

Another EW option for the MiG-35/D could be a variation of the L-175M Khibiny which is normally housed in wingtip mounted pods on aircraft such as the Su-35S or Su-34, but would have to be accommodated in new pods on underwing stations or potentially on new designed lumps and bumps on the airframe.

Among the foreign equipment that can be integrated on the MiG-35 is the Elettronica S.p.As ELT/568(V)2, active jamming station. This system is made up of a pair of HF emitters in the main section which would be fitted in the aft bay in the cockpit with other antennas located in the LERX's and a further element of the system located in the rear fuselage with the antenna housed below the rudder of the starboard vertical tail. This system was apparently specified for the MiG-35/D bid in the Indian MMRCA (Medium Multi-Role Combat Aircraft) competition.

The Elettronica description of the ELT/568 reads "The ELT/568 system is a modular family designed for self/mutual protection of combat aircraft.

During flight operations, ELT.568 detects radar signals and transmits jamming signals according to the RWR designation with which it is integrated or, in 'Stand-Alone' mode, can operate independently, according to library loaded before the mission.

A series of communication channel (BUS 1553) and lines for discrete signals are designed to manage compatibility/integration with other on-board RX and TX devices.

The different versions of ELT/568 allow to manage from 4 simultaneous threats (where 2 can have high transmission duty) up to 16 threats, according to the relevant transmitted unit (TWT or Solid State) and antennas configuration (Antenna Array are also provided)."

Disposable elements of the self-defence suite consist of a battery of Chaff/flare dispensers for defence against radar homing and infrared homing missiles respectively.

The NPP Zvezda PAZ-MK in-flight refueling unit developed for the naval MiG-29K/KUB can be employed by the MiG-35/D, allowing the aircraft to refuel other aircraft in flight. NPP Zvezda

Neither RAC or its parent company UAC have released performance specifications for the MiG-35/D, although some figures, very limited in detail, do appear in Rosoboronexport documentation, although these appear more akin to figures derived from the MiG-29K/KUB rather than the MiG-29M/M2 with which the MiG-35/D shares more commonality, casting some superficial doubt on the Rosoboronexport figures, which have not been confirmed by either RAC or UAC.

RAC figures show the MiG-29K/KUB to have a maximum speed of 1400 km/h at sea level while the MiG-29M/M2 has a sea level maximum speed of 1500 km/h. Rosoboronexport states the maximum speed of the MiG-35/D at sea level as 1400 km/h, although it would be logical to assume that the value was more akin to the 1500 km/h of the MiG-29M/M2. RAC figures for the MiG-29K/KUB maximum speed at upper altitude are 2200 km/h and 2100 km/h respectively, these values being significantly lower than the value of 2400 km/h released by RAC for the MiG-29M/M2. Rosoboronexport states that the maximum speed at upper altitude for the MiG-35/D is 2100 km/h, in-line with the MiG-29KUB, although these figures should be taken with a degree of caution as the MiG-35/D is more likely to have a maximum speed more akin to that of the MiG-29M/M2, maximum Mach number for this variant being confirmed as 2.25 by RAC.

The PAZ-MK in-flight refueling unit would be carried on the fuselage centre station as demonstrated by this MiG-29KUB refueling a MiG-29UPG.

Figures released by RAC show the MiG-29K/KUB and MiG-29M/M2 to have a ceiling of 17500 m, it being reasonable therefore to infer that this value would correspond to the ceiling of the MiG-35/D. RAC figures show the MiG-29K to have a g-load limit of +8 while the load limit for the MiG-29M/M2 is stated as +9, it being reasonable to infer this value for the MiG-35/D, which would correspond with the Rosoboronexport figures of +9 to -3.

The basic kinetic and load limit performance parameters of the MiG-29M/M2, which, assuming some inaccuracy in the Rosoboronexport figures, should correspond to the performance parameters of the MiG-35/D, are similar to those of the MiG-29SE, based on the first generation MiG-29 airframe, with the same values for maximum speed at sea level, upper altitude, maximum Mach number and g-load limit. The MiG-29SE has a slightly increased ceiling, but is vastly inferior in range which stands at 2100 km configured with three external fuel tanks, this being 1100 km lower than the value for the MiG-29M and 1000 km lower than the value for the MiG-29M2, the figures for the MiG-35/D being assumed to be similar to the latter.

One of the major design goals of the Unified Fighter Family was to address the chronic short range problem inherent in the first generation MiG-29. To this end, internal fuel capacity in the MiG-29K/KUB/M/M2 and MiG-35/D was increased over that of the first generation airframe. The rear cockpit compartment of all three variants is able to accommodate an additional fuel tank in the single seat models, MiG-29K, MiG-29M and MiG-35.

The MiG-35D demonstrator, Blue 154, with upper fuselage mounted airbrake deployed. RAC

Range figures released by RAC for the MiG-29M on a ferry mission stand at 2000 km without external fuel tanks and 3200 km with three external fuel tanks; the values for the MiG-29M2 being 1800 km and 3000 km respectively. The figure of 6000 km is given for a MiG-29M/M2 ferry mission with three external fuel tanks and one in-flight refueling. It could be inferred that these values correspond to the same values for the MiG-35/D. That said, Rosoboronexport documentation states a MiG-35/D value of 5700 km for the latter scenario. The MiG-29K/KUB has slightly reduced range values at 2000 km and 1700 km without external fuel tanks respectively; 3000 km and 2700 km with three external fuel tanks respectively and 5500 km for both variants with three external fuel tanks and one in-flight refueling.

Range for all variants can be further increased through additional in-flight refuelling's. The MiG-35/D retractable in-flight refueling probe, located just ahead of the windscreen on the port side forward fuselage, is thought to be the same ATG-2E system employed by the MiG-29K/KUB/MiG-29SMT and Sukhoi's stable of $4^{th}+/4^{th}++$ generation multirole combat aircraft, the Su-30MKI/SM and Su-35S.

The MiG-35 is compatible with the PAZ-MK in-flight refueling unit developed for the naval MiG-29K/KUB allowing the aircraft to refuel other aircraft in-flight. The length of the hose that is streamed from the unit is 18.5 m, the hose inner diameter being 52 mm; the system, which is controlled by a digital control system featuring various operating modes, including displaying system status, being capable of transferring fuel at up to 750 l/min to a receiver aircraft.

Page 59-68: The MiG-35D demonstrator Blue 154. RAC

MiG-35/D in model form at the Dubai Air trade show. RAC and UAC are actively marketing the MiG-35/D with interest in the design being shown in several market areas, particularly North Africa and the Middle East. Whether or not this interest transforms to firm orders, only time will tell. RAC

The Russian Federation Air Force has a requirement for modern MiG-29 derivatives to replace at least part of its fleet of first generation MiG-29 fighter aircraft. The replacement process has been implemented piecemeal with a token number of MiG-29SMT/Upgraded UB fighters being procured in the late 2000's; these aircraft having originally been ordered and then cancelled by Algeria. The MODRF (Ministry of Defence of the Russian Federation) ordered an additional 16

MiG-29SMT multi-role fighters on 14 April 2014, these aircraft, which were assembled at RAC MiG No.2 Production facility, Moscow, were scheduled to be delivered between late 2015 and through 2016, bringing to 46 the number of modern MiG-29's in Russian Federation Air Force service. In addition Phazotron revealed in 2012 that it was to upgrade the radar systems in the Russian Air Force fleet of MiG-29SMT fighters, although whether this would include the incorporation of an AESA was undisclosed.

The Russian Federation Air Force was expected to be the launch customer for the MiG-35/D, but the expected contract signing has been delayed several times. As of December 2015, RAC expected to sign a contract for the supply of MiG-35/D fighters to the Russian Federation Air Force sometime in 2016/2017, the aircraft to be delivered from 2018-2020 according to the Russian Federation Air Force Commander in Chief Victor Bondarev, assuming of course such an order does materialise.

For several years past, Egypt has expressed an interest in Russian $4^{th}+/4^{th}++$ multirole combat aircraft, interest in the MiG-35/D being confirmed in late summer 2015. In early 2016, it was confirmed that Egypt was in negotiations with Russia regarding a potential MiG-35/D purchase with in excess of 40 aircraft unofficially being expressed as the number of such aircraft required.

India was long touted as the likely launch customer for the MiG-35/D, several phases of a competition with other foreign competitors being progressed through in that nations MMRCA competition designed to replace older aircraft types in the Indian Air Force inventory. The MiG-35/D, however, was dropped from the competition, which has at least partially been filled by a purchase of Dassault Rafale multirole (Omni-role) fighter aircraft from France.

It was the need to field additional aircraft in the extensive trials/demonstration program for the Indian MMRCA competition that led to RAC increasing its stable of demonstrator's from the single MiG-35D, Blue 154, which was converted from a MiG-29KUB prototype, flying as the MiG-35D in 2007, to three such aircraft by adding MiG-35D code 967 and MiG-35 code 961, the former of the two apparently being converted from MiG-29KUB prototype, 947, during 2009.

4

ADVANCED WEAPONS OPTIONS

The MiG-35/D can be armed with a wide diversity of radar and infrared homing air to air missiles and guided and unguided air to surface munitions. As is the case with the MiG-29M/M2, the MiG-35/D appears to have nine external stores stations; the oft stated ten stations including the so called next generation optoelectronic fairing located on the starboard engine trunk. Maximum external stores load is 6500 kg in all cases. In addition to ordnance the stores stations can be used for the carriage of external fuel tanks and sensors pods such as the Sapsan-E optoelectronics pod.

The fixed armament consists of a single Gsh-301 30 mm cannon located in the port side fuselage/wing root with accommodation for 150 rounds of ammunition. This weapon can fire at a rate of between 1500 and 1800 rounds per minute, with a muzzle velocity of 870 meters per second. The cannon has a range out to around 1800 meters in the air to air role or up to 800 meters against surface targets. For air to air and air to surface missions the cannon is primarily a secondary weapon.

The MiG-35/D can be armed with the Kh-31A anti-ship missile and the Kh-31P anti-radiation missile, a total of four of any one kind or a mix of both variants able to be accommodated; the missiles being carried one on each of the two innermost wing stations. Documentation provided by JSC Tactical Missiles Corporation shows that the Kh-31P features "changeable passive radar homing heads... operating in corresponding frequency bands" allowing it to engage "modern continuous-wave and pulsed radar" employed by medium and long range surface to air missile systems. The missile can also engage other emitting radar not necessarily part of the air defence network. The homing head autonomously searches for and locks-on to a target, or, alternatively, the aircraft sensors can hand down targeting information to the missile before it is launched from the AKU-58 airborne ejection unit.

The Kh-31P, which has a launch weight of around 600 kg, has a length of 4.7 m, 0.36 m diameter and has a wing span of 0.914 m, can be launched from altitudes of 100 m to 15000 m at a carrier speed of Mach 0.65 to Mach 1.25, after which it flies to targets between 15 to 110 km away (depending upon launch altitude) at speeds of 1000 m/s. The target is destroyed by an 87 kg high explosive fragmentation warhead.

The MiG-35/D and other members of the Unified Fighter Family can employ a diversity of modern air to air and air to surface missiles as shown on this Unified Fighter Family model at Le Bourget, Paris, in June 2015. RAC

A modified variant of the missile, designated Kh-31PK, employs a larger warhead that is detonated by a proximity fuse. This variant retains the same operating parameters to those of the Kh-31P. The Kh-31PD is an evolution of the Kh-31P, range being increased from a maximum of 110 km to 250 km whilst carrying a more powerful warhead.

As with the Kh-31P, the MiG-35/D can carry up to four Kh-31A anti-ship missiles. Developed as a high-speed air launched anti-ship missile, the Kh-31A is designed to engage warships operating independently or as part of a larger integrated naval group. The missile, which has the same overall dimensions, similar launch weight, and identical launch parameters as the Kh-31P, can be launched from the carrier aircraft singly or in salvo in clear and adverse weather conditions, against background clutter in an active jamming environment. The missiles on-board active-radar homing head can designate targets in both pre-and-post launch modes and conduct target acquisition and selection, and, as stated in JSC Tactical Missiles Corporation documentation, determines "target coordinates (range, azimuth, elevation), generation of command signals", which are fed directly to the guidance system. The missile is carried on and launched from the AKU-58A ejection unit, cruising at a speed of 1000 m/s to targets 5 to 70 km distant (against a Destroyer size target) depending on launch altitude. The target is then destroyed or disabled by the 95 kg warhead.

The Kh-31AD is an evolution of the Kh-31A with many improvements, including a 15% more powerful warhead and longer range; the latter being more than twice that of the Kh-31A.

The Unified Fighter Family higher external stores load can be carried on eight external stores stations on the MiG-29K/KUB or nine on the MiG-29M/M2/MiG-35/D. RAC

Another anti-ship missile integrated with the MiG-35/D is the Kh-35E, four of which can be carried; one on each of the two innermost wing stations on each wing. This weapon, which is designed to destroy surface vessels, including warships displacing up to 5,000 tonnes, can be launched from warships (Uran-E ship-borne missile system), coastal missile batteries (Bal-E mobile coastal launch system) and aircraft launched. The aircraft launched missile has a length of 3.85 m, diameter 0.42 m, wing span 1.33 m and a launch weight of 520 kg.

Once launched from the mother aircraft, with maximum turn angle in horizontal plane after launch of ±90°, the missile, which cruises at Mach 0.8, descends to an altitude of some 10 to 15 m above the sea surface, dropping to 4 m for the terminal phase of the flight, to strike targets up to 130 km distant in sea states up to 6 in an active electronic countermeasures environment; the ARGS-35E active radar seeker having an acquisition range of around 20 km, thereafter the target is locked-on and destroyed or disabled by the 145 kg high explosive penetrator warhead.

The Kh-35UE improves on the Kh-35E in a number of areas, including range, which is doubled from 130 km to 260 km, and features an improved post-launch horizontal turn capability.

The MiG-35/D can be armed with the Kh-31A anti-ship missile (above) and the Kh-31P anti-radiation missile. Author **Enhancements to the Kh-31 weapons led to the Kh-31AD anti-ship missile and the Kh-31PD anti-radiation missile (above).** JSC Tactical Missiles Corporation

The standard battlefield air to surface missiles cleared on the MiG-35/D are the Kh-29TE(L), which are short range air to surface weapons, four of which can be carried on the same stations as used for the carriage of the Kh-31 and Kh-35.

The Kh-29 was designed for use against hardened targets such as large bridges, reinforced runways, industrial centres and aircraft housed in hardened aircraft shelters, and can also be employed effectively against surface vessels with a displacement up to 10,000 tons. The Kh-29 missiles, which are 3.9 m in length, 0.4 m diameter, 1.1 m wing span and have a launch weight of 690 kg for the Kh-29TE and 660 kg for the Kh-29L, are carried on and launched from AKU-58AE airborne ejector units; the Kh-29TE being guided to the target by a passive TV guidance system whilst the Kh-29L is fitted with a semi-active laser guidance system; the target being destroyed by the 320 kg high explosive penetrating warhead. JSC Tactical Missiles Corporation documentation shows the missile to have a minimum engagement range of 3 km and a maximum engagement range of 2 to 30 km for the Kh-29TE (depending on launch altitude) and 10 km for the Kh-29L.

The MiG-35/D can be armed with the Kh-29TE/L short range air to surface missile shown above with a MiG-29SM demonstrator. Author.

The MiG-35/D is cleared to operate with a number of guided bomb units of the KAB-500 series with four KAB-500Kr(OD) weapons able to be accommodated one on each of the two innermost stations on both wings. The KAB-500 weapons have launch weights of 520 kg (500Kr) and 370 kg (500-OD) with a warhead weight of 380 kg and 250 kg respectively. The weapons, which are 3.05 m in length with a 0.35 m diameter and can be released from altitudes of 0.5 to 5 km at carrier speeds of 550 to 1100 km/h, have a root mean square deviation of 4-7 m, the target being destroyed by the concrete piercing high explosive penetrator warhead in in the KAB-500Kr or the high explosive fuel air warhead in the KAB-500-OD.

It is unclear if the larger KAB-1500 series such as the KAB-500Kr, which has a launch weight of 1525 kg, can be carried. If so, then this weapon, which has a warhead weight of 1170 kg, would only be carried on the innermost wings stations. Launch parameters for this weapon are 1 to 8 km altitude and 550 to 1100 km/h carrier speed with a root mean square deviation of 4-7 m.

The KAB-500 series (left of photograph) are specified as the baseline guided bomb units for the Unified Fighter Family, including the MiG-35/D. It is unclear if the MiG-35/D, or indeed other members of the Unified Fighter Family, will be able to operate with the larger KAB-1500 series (right of photograph). Author

As shown by this image of the MiG-35D demonstrator, Blue 154, the MiG-35/D is expected to be cleared for operation with not only the medium range RVV-AE and short-range R-73E air to air missiles, but also the medium range R-27ER1 SARH and possibly the R-27ET1 passive infrared homing air to air missiles. RAC

In the air to air role the MiG-35/D can be armed with the standard Russian medium and short-range air to air weapons; the Vympel (JSC Tactical Missiles Corporation) R-27ER1(R1), R-27ET1(T1), RVV-AE and R-73E (in Russian language the weapons are P-27, P-73 or K-27, K-73). In the case of the R-27 variants, these are not specifically mentioned in RAC armament lists, the RVV-AE being the major beyond visual range air to air missile specified. However, the R-27, which has flown in aerodynamic missile form on the MiG-35D demonstrator, is expected to form a part of the armament options for export aircraft, and, ccertainly for any MiG-35/D purchase for the Russian Federation Air Force the full spectrum of R-27 variants are expected to be employed with the possible exception of the R-27EP1(P1) air to air anti-radiation missile.

Entering service in the mid-1980's as the primary air to air armament of the MiG-29 and Su-27, the R-27 medium-range missile variants in service in 2015 are more capable updates of the R-27, of which a whole family of variants was produced, including the R-27R1, NATO reporting name AA-10 'Alamo' A with SARH (Semi-Active Radar Homing) guidance and the R-27T1 'Alamo' B with IR guidance. Longer range variants were also developed, designated R-27ER1 for the SARH variant and R-27ET1 for the passive infrared homing variant. These missiles, 'Alamo' C and 'Alamo' D respectively, are fitted with a boost sustain motor to extend engagement range. Two R-27ER1(R1) or R-27ET1(T1) missiles can be carried by the MiG-35/D on the innermost wing stations.

The MiG-35/D is expected to operate with the R-27ER1 SARH medium range air to air missile. Author

The R-27ER1 has a length of 4.775 m, diameter 0.26 m at solid rocket motor section and 0.23 m at control unit section, wing span of 0.803 m and control plane span of 0.972 m. The R-27ET1 dimensions are the same as those of the R-27ER1 with the exception of length which is slightly reduced at 4.49 m. The R-27ER1 has a launch weight of 350 kg whilst the R-27ET1 launch weight is slightly lower at 343 kg. Missile flight speed is Mach 4, the R-27ER1 having an engagement range of 60 to 62.5 km against a fighter aircraft size target and up to 100 km when used against larger targets such as an AWACS (Airborne Warning and Control System) platform. The infrared guided R-27ET1 has an engagement range of 80 km against a target in the front hemisphere. Both variants are armed with a 39 kg expanding rod warhead.

Complementing the larger infrared guided R-27ET1 is the smaller, shorter range, but highly agile, Vympel (JSC Tactical Missiles Corporation) R-73E (NATO reporting name AA-11 'Archer') infrared homing missile, eight of which can be carried by the MiG-35/D; one on each of the four wing stations on each wing.

When it entered service in the 1980's, the R-73 was probably the most advanced short-range air to air missile in the world, being a generation ahead of the latest variants of the American AIM-9L/M Sidewinder or European Matra Magic 2 short-range infrared guided air to air missiles then arming NATO fighters. Only in the early 21st century did NATO field comparable systems in the shape of the MBDA (Matra British Aerospace Dynamics Alenia) ASRAAM (Advanced Short Range Air to Air Missile) and Raytheon AIM-9X Evolved Sidewinder.

The R-73E (above) and its replacement, the RVV-MD, which is a modernised evolution of the R-73E, will constitute the standard Russian short-range infrared guided air to air missiles for the next several decades. Author

The R-73 was developed with high agility as a design driver, augmented by the ability of the pilot of the MiG-29 or Su-27 fighters to cue the weapon to targets at up to 60° off-boresight via a HPS (Helmet Pointing System). High manoeuvrability was achieved by a combination of a number of factors, including four forward control fins, elevators attached to the rear fins, which are fixed, and deflector vanes positioned in the nozzle of the rocket engine.

The R-73E has a length of 2.9 m, diameter 0.17 m, wing span 0.51 m and control plane span of 0.38 m, launch weight being 105 kg. The missile, which has a longer reach than most western equivalents such as the many AIM-9 variants, has a maximum engagement range of 30 km against a head-on target and a minimum engagement range of 0.3 km against a tail-on target manoeuvring at up to 12 g. Missiles can be launched at altitudes from 0.02 km up to 20 km, the all-aspect passive infrared seeker head guiding the missile to the target, which would then be destroyed by the 8 kg expanding rod warhead.

Up to six RVV-AE active radar guided medium range air to air missiles can be carried by the MiG-35/D on the three innermost stations on each wing. Development of this weapon apparently commenced in 1982 and the missile began entering limited service in the mid-1990's, certainly with trials units in Russia. Into the 21st century the weapon has been integrated onto a number of aircraft types undergoing updates as well as new aircraft of the Su-27SM3, Su-30, Su-34, Su-35S, and MiG-29 variants, as well as the Sukhoi T-50 PAK FA fifth generation multirole fighter aircraft. The weapon has also been exported to a number of customers.

The JSC Tactical Missiles Corporation RVV-AE active radar guided medium range air to air missile is the standard medium range air to air missile offered to domestic and export customers operating modern and upgraded Russian tactical combat aircraft. An evolution of the missile, the RVV-SD, is the current planned replacement, although other advanced air to air missiles are being developed in Russia. Author

The RVV-AE has narrow-span wings of rectangular shape and four lattice control surfaces at the rear; among the benefits of this type of control surface being reduced flow-separation at high angle of attack. Basic dimensions of the RVV-AE are length 3.6 m, diameter 0.2 m, wingspan 0.4 m and control plane span 0.7 m. The standard RVV-AE, which has a launch weight of 175 kg, has a minimum engagement range of 0.3 km in the rear hemisphere and a maximum range of 80 km in the forward hemisphere, apparently reaches speeds of Mach 4 and can engage targets manoeuvring at up to 12 g from 0.2 to 25 km altitude.

The designer noted that while the RVV-AE is heavier than the US Raytheon AIM-120A/C AMRAAM (Advanced Medium Range Air to Air Missile) and the European MICA EM, the Russian missile has a longer range and better performance when engaging manoeuvring targets compared to its western rivals. Like its western rivals the RVV-AE can be employed in a launch-and-forget mode and features a multi-stage guidance system that includes inertial command in the initial phase with mid-course updates via an aircraft to missile datalink for long-range engagements, with active radar homing in the terminal phase of the engagement. The on-board active-radar apparently has an acquisition-range of around 20 km. The missile, which features an active-radar fuse for the 22.5 kg warhead, can apparently be used in a 'self-defence' mode to intercept missiles launched at the mother aircraft, although how effective this capability is, or if indeed such a capability is viable for the technology involved, is unclear.

The MiG-35D demonstrator, Blue 154, with a load of two KAB-500 series guided bomb units, four RVV-AE medium range air to air missiles and a pair of R-73E short-range air to air missiles. RAC

As well as the weapons specified, the MiG-35/D can have other weapons integrated such as the Kh-38 family of battlefield tactical missiles that have been specified for the 5th generation Sukhoi T-50 PAK FA. Although not specified in released documentation, it is possible that the LGB-250 smart bomb will be integrated with the MiG-35/D should it enter Russian Federation Air Force service.

Although not specified in released documentation, it is expected that the RVV-MD and RVV-SD, respective replacements for the R-73E and RVV-AE, will be integrated with the MiG-35/D. An evolution of the R-73, the RVV-MD is a new generation highly agile infrared guided missile developed to arm the new generation of Russian 4th+4th++ and 5th generation fighter aircraft. The JSC Tactical Missiles Corporation description states the "short range missile for close high manoeuvrable air combat provides hitting air targets (fighters, bombers, combat aircrafts, military aircrafts and helicopters), day and night, at all angles, on background of earth, under active enemy counteraction." The missile, which is powered by a single mode engine, features enhanced anti-jamming protection over its forebear, including optical jamming, and, according to JSC Tactical Missiles Corporation documentation, features "all angles passive infrared target homing (double range individual homing) with combined aero-gas dynamics control." The target is destroyed by a rod-shaped warhead activated by a laser non-contact sensor fuse in the RVV-MDL or a radio non-contact sensor in the RVV-MD. The weapon is carried on and launched from the P-72-1D (P-72-1BD2) type rail tracked launcher.

The RVV-SD, developed by JSC Tactical Missiles Corporation, is clearly an evolution of the RVV-AE incorporating a number of improvements over its forebear, with longer engagement range, increased engagement capability and enhanced resistance to electronic countermeasures. JSC Tactical Missiles Corporation describes the missile as "intended for hitting air targets (fighters, bombers, attack aircraft, helicopters… cruise missiles) day and night, at all angles, under electronic countermeasures, on background of earth and water surfaces, including multichannel application 'fire-and-forget'". The missile, which is powered by a single mode rocket engine, incorporates inertial homing "with radar correction and active radar self-homing". The target is destroyed by a rod-shaped multi-charge warhead with detonation by laser non-contact target sensor. For external carriage on 4th+, 4th++ and 5th generation aircraft the missile is carried on and launched from the AKU-170E missile ejection launcher.

The MiG-35/D, as is the case with other members of the Unified Fighter Family, is expected to be able to employ a number of unguided bomb types such as the FAB-500 (ZB-500, RBK-500, and BetAB-500) general purpose bombs; the smaller FAB-250 (OFAB-250-270) general purpose bombs or OFAB-100-120 general purpose bombs.

Unguided rockets are expected to include up to four B-8M-1 rocket pods; two on each of the innermost wing stations or four smaller B-13L rocket pods can be carried on the same stations. Another alternative is four S-25, S-250OFM-PU rockets which are carried on the same stations as the B-8M-1 and B-13L.

APPENDICES

Appendix I

The in-house design code for the MiG-29K/KUB has been referred to as 9-41 while that of the MiG-35/D has been referred to as the 9-61: these designations being based on their respective side codes, Blue 154 of the MiG-35D demonstrator aside. However, attempts to have these codes confirmed by RAC were unsuccessful, therefore they may be subject to change in the future.

Appendix II

The specification for the MiG-29M/M2 is inferred to be, for the most part, representative of the MiG-35/D for which no official figures have been released. No weight figures have been released for either the MiG-35/D or the MiG-29M/M2, but for the former these are expected to be in the region of 23500 kg.

RAC data for the MiG-29M/M2 (M2 figures are in brackets)

Length: 17.3 m
Height: 4.4 m
Wing span: 11.99 m
Normal take-off weight: 17500 kg (17800 kg)
Maximum airspeed: 1500 km/h at sea level, 2400 km/h at altitude
Maximum Mach number: 2.25
Service ceiling: 17500 m
Maximum g-load: 9
Ferry range: 2000 km without external fuel tanks (1800 km); 3200 km with three external fuel tanks (3000 km); 6000 km with three external fuel tanks and one in-flight refueling
Engines: Two x RD-33MK each rated at 9000 kg for take-off
External stores station: 9
Weapon load: the external stores load of 6500 kg carried on nine external stores stations can include various combinations. Maximum 6 x RVV-AE; maximum 8 x R-73E; maximum 4 x Kh-29T(TE); maximum 4 x Kh-31A; maximum 4 x Kh-35E; maximum 4 x Kh-31P; maximum 4 x KAB-500Kr guided bombs. The fixed armament consists of a single Gsh-301 cannon with 150 rounds of ammunition (this capacity may be subject to change in series production aircraft). As well as ordnance the aircraft can carry up to three external fuel tanks or other stores such as the Sapsan-E optoelectronic pod.

Appendix III

RAC data for the MiG-29 Ver. B, figures in brackets refer for the most part to the MiG-29UB (provided for comparison with the Unified Fighter Family)

Length: 17.32 m (17.42 m for the MiG-29UB)
Height: 4.73 m
Wing span: 11.36 m
Standard take-off weight: 14900 kg (14600 kg for the MiG-29UB)
Maximum take-off weight: 18000 kg (18200 kg for the MiG-29UB)
Maximum airspeed: 1500 km/h at sea level, 2400 km/h at upper altitude (2230 km/k MiG-29UB) at upper altitude
Maximum Mach number: 2.35 (2.1 MiG-29UB)
Service ceiling: 18000 m (17500 MiG-29UB)
Maximum g-load: 9
Ferry range: 1500 km without external fuel tanks (1450 km MiG-29UB); 2000 km with one external fuel tank (2000 km MiG-29UB); (2900 km with three external fuel tanks MiG-29SE)
Engines: Two x RD-33 SER.2(3) each rated at 8300 kg for take-off
External stores station: 6
Weapon load: can include various combinations. Maximum 6 x RVV-AE; maximum 8 x R-73E; maximum 4 x Kh-29T(TE); maximum 4 x Kh-31A; maximum 4 x Kh-35E; maximum 4 x Kh-31P; maximum 4 x KAB-500Kr guided bombs.
Cannon: Gsh-301

Appendix IV

Comparison of basic performance parameters of the Unified Fighter Family variants with a first generation airframe variant – the MiG-29SE

	K	KUB	M	M2	35	35D	SE
Normal weight:	18550	18650	17500	17800			15300
Max take-off weight:	24500	24500			23500	23500	20000
Speed sea level:	1400	1400	1500	1500	1400	1400	1500
Speed altitude:	2200	2100	2400	2400	2100	2100	2400
Mach Number:			2.25	2.25			2.25
Ceiling:	17500	17500	17500	17500			17750
g-load:	8	8	9	9	+9/-3	+9/-3	9
Ferry Range (km)							
no EFT:	2000	1700	2000	1800			1500[A]
with 3 EFT:	3000	2700	3200	3000			2100[B]
3 EFT and 1 refuel:	5500	5500	6000	6000	6000	5700	2900[C]
External stations:	8	8	9	9	9	9	6

A = No EFT (External Fuel Tank); B = 1 EFT, C = 3 EFT and no in-flight refueling (refuel)

GLOSSARY

AMRAAM	Advanced Medium Range Air to Air Missile
AoA	Angle of Attack
ASRAAM	Advanced Short Range Air to Air Missile
AWACS	Airborne Warning and Control System
CIS	Commonwealth of Independent States
dB	Decibel
DoD	Department of Defence
DRFM	Digital Radio Frequency Memory
ECM	Electronic Counter Measures
ESM	Electronic Sensor Measures
EW	Electronic Warfare
F	Fighter
FADEC	Full Authority Digital Engine Control
FBW	Fly By Wire
FCS	Flight Control System
FOD	Foreign Object Damage
FX	Fighter Experimental
GPS	Global Positioning System
h	hour
H	Height
HF	
HMTDIS	Helmet Mounted Target Designation and Indication System
HMTDS	Helmet Mounted Target Designation System
HOTAS	Hands on Throttle and Stick
HPS	Helmet Pointing System
HUD	Heads Up Display
IA-PVO	*Istrebitelnaya Aviatsiya Protivo-Vozdushnoy Obstrany*/Air Defence Force
IFF	Identification Friend or Foe
IRST	Infrared Search and Track
IRST/LR	Infrared Search and Track/Laser Range
JSC	Joint Stock Company
kg	Kilogram
kgf	Kilogram force
KLITV	Klimov Thrust Vector
km	Kilometer
km/h	Kilometer per hour
Kret	JSC Concern Radio-Electronic Technologies
LERX	Leading Edge Root Extensions
LFI	*Legikiy Frontovoy Istrebitel* – Light Front line Fighter
LR	Laser Range
m	metre

m/s	metres per second
MBDA	Matra British Aerospace Dynamics Alenia
MFDS	Multi-Functional Display Screen
MiG	Mikoyan
MMRCA	Medium Multi-Role Combat Aircraft
Mrad	Milliradian - Unit of angular measurement (1000 mrad = 1 radian)
MRCA	Multi-Role Combat Aircraft
MTBF	Man Time Between Failure
NATO	North Atlantic Treaty Organisation
ODN	Omni-Directional Nozzle
OLS	Optical Location Station (System)
ORS	Optical Radar Station
PAK FA	*Perspektivniy Aviacionniy Complex Frontovoi Aviacii* – Perspective Aviation Complex for Front line Aviation
PFI	Advanced Front Line Fighter
PIRATE	Passive Infrared Airborne Tracking Equipment
RAC	Russian Aircraft Corporation
RF	Radio Frequency
RPBK	JSC Ramenskoye Design Bureau
RWR	Radar Warning Receiver
SARH	Semi-Active Radar Homing
Su	Sukhoi
T/R	Transmit/Receive
TVN	Thrust Vector Nozzle
UAC	United Aircraft Corporation
US	United States
USAF	United States Air Force
V	Velocity
V_E	Velocity
WCS	Weapon Control System
°	Degrees
±	Plus or minus
<	Strict inequality – Less than

ABOUT THE AUTHOR

Hugh, a historian and author, has published in excess of sixty books; non-fiction and fiction, writing under his given name as well as utilising two different pseudonyms. He has also written for several international magazines, whilst his work has been used as reference for many other projects ranging from the aviation industry, international news corporations and film media to encyclopaedias, museum exhibits and the computer gaming industry. He currently resides in his native Scotland

Other titles by the author include

Sukhoi T-50/PAK FA - Russia's 5th Generation 'Stealth' Fighter
Sukhoi Su-35S 'Flanker' E - Russia's 4++ Generation Super-Manoeuvrability Fighter
Sukhoi Su-34 'Fullback'
Sukhoi Su-30MKK/MK2/M2 - Russo Kitashiy Striker from Amur
Eurofighter Typhoon - Storm over Europe
Tornado F.2/F.3 Air Defence Variant
Air to Air Missile Directory
North American F-108 Rapier - Mach 3 Interceptor
Convair YB-60 - Fort Worth Overcast
Boeing X-36 Tailless Agility Flight Research Aircraft
X-32 - The Boeing Joint Strike Fighter
X-35 - Progenitor to the F-35 Lightning II
X-45 Uninhabited Combat Air Vehicle
Into The Cauldron - The Lancaster MK.I Daylight Raid on Augsburg
Light Battle Cruisers and the Second Battle of Heligoland Bight
British Battlecruisers of World War 1 - Operational Log, July 1914-June 1915
Hurricane IIB Combat Log - 151 Wing RAF, North Russia 1941
RAF Meteor Jet Fighters in World War II, an Operational Log
Typhoon IA/B Combat Log - Operation Jubilee, August 1942
Defiant MK.I Combat Log - Fighter Command, May-September 1940
Blenheim MK.IF Combat Log - Fighter Command Day Fighter Sweeps/Night
Interceptions, September 1939 - June 1940
Tomahawk I/II Combat Log - European Theatre, 1941-42
Fortress MK.I Combat Log - Bomber Command High Altitude Bombing
Operations, July-September 1941
F-84 Thunderjet - Republic Thunder
USAF Jet Powered Fighters - XP-59-XF-85
XF-92 - Convairs Arrow